Antiques

Rachael Feild

GUINNESS BOOKS

EDITOR: Beatrice Frei
DESIGN AND LAYOUT: Alan Hamp and Mandy Sedge

© Rachael Feild and Guinness Publishing Ltd, 1986, 1990
Second edition © 1988
Third edition © 1990

Published in Great Britain by Guinness Publishing Ltd,
33 London Road, Enfield, Middlesex

Typeset in England by
Dorchester Typesetting Group Ltd

Printed and bound in Portugal by Printer Portuguesa

'Guinness' is a registered trade mark of
Guinness Superlatives Ltd

British Library Cataloguing in Publication Data

Feild, Rachael
    Guinness antiques: price guide – 3rd ed.
    1.   Antiques. Collecting
    I.   Title   II.   Feild, Rachael. Antiques pocket price guide
    745.1′075

ISBN 0-85112-394-5

Contents

Acknowledgements 4

Introduction 7

Chronological chart 14

FURNITURE 17

CLOCKS 97

SILVER 133

POTTERY AND PORCELAIN 175

GLASS 237

Glossary 267

Bibliography 283

Index 285

ACKNOWLEDGEMENTS

The publisher would like to thank Phillips Fine Art Auctioneers for the use of all the photographs in this book. Michael Cowley, Christopher Greenwood, Michael Prevezer and Douglas Wright for their help in updating the prices in this edition; Jacqueline Barber (photographic research) and John Sandon for the introduction to the English pottery and porcelain section.

RACHAEL FEILD has spent most of her working life in magazines and journalism. Her first book, written in collaboration with Rupert Gentle, was the definitive *English Domestic Brass 1680–1810*. She has contributed to many of the major antiques magazines including a series of articles for *Connoisseur*. Rachael Feild is the author of the *Which? Guide to Buying Antiques* published by The Consumers' Association, *Irons in the Fire* – a History of Cooking Equipment published by Crowood Press and *Buying Antique Furniture* published by Macdonald which featured in the *Sunday Times* bestseller list. She has also contributed a regular monthly feature on prices and trends in the London and provincial salerooms for *Antique Dealer & Collectors' Guide* as well as many other articles on specialist subjects.

Phillips
Fine Art Auctioneers

PHILLIPS FINE ART Auctioneers have the largest and most comprehensive network of salerooms throughout the British Isles, with 33 saleroom branches offering a full range of services, from Scotland to Cornwall, Wales to East Anglia. Each regional office is self-contained and is run on individual lines, with regular sales calendars for antiques and objets d'art from the surrounding area. It is not Phillips' policy to cream off the best objects to send down to their London salerooms, except on rare occasions when, in their capacity as agents for the vendors, they consider that a better price would be obtained. This is by no means the rule, since many regions have built up their own specialist sales which are regularly attended by important collectors and private buyers from all over the country. Thus every region has the full benefit of Phillips' expertise and can be assured of the highest standards of service to both buyer and seller. In addition, Phillips hold regular road shows when teams of experts visit towns and cities to advise and value an incredibly wide range of antiques and objets d'art brought to them by members of the public.

Phillips were established in 1796: many of their regional salerooms are continuations of even older firms of fine art auctioneers which have now become members of the Phillips group, using the same strict conditions of sale and maintaining the same high standards of practice. In recent years, Phillips has built up many of the smaller specialist categories into sales of considerable importance, particularly with their collectors' sales at Phillips West Two in Bayswater, London.

The wide and varied range of more regular items can be seen in the pages of this Pocket Guide. All illustrations have been carefully chosen from Phillips' extensive photographic library of objects which have passed through their salerooms in the last two years – a small representation of the 101 million turnover achieved in 1989. Phillips also have a comprehensive coverage of the international field and have branches in New York, Brussels, Geneva, Netherlands, Paris, Toronto and Zurich, with representatives in Australia, West Germany and Portugal.

Phillips
FINE ART AUCTIONEERS & VALUERS SINCE 1796

Blenstock House

SALEROOMS

Phillips – London
101 New Bond Street,
London W1Y 0AS
Tel: 01-629 6602
Telex: 298855 Blen G
Fax: 01-629 8876

Marylebone
Hayes Place,
Lisson Grove,
London NW1 6UA
Tel: 01-723 2647

West 2
10 Salem Road,
Bayswater W2 4DL
Tel: 01-229 9090
Fax: 01-792 9201

Glendining's
101 New Bond Street,
London W1Y 9LD
Tel: 01-493 2445
Fax: 01-491 9181

Phillips – Bath
1 Old King Street,
Bath BA1 2JT
Tel: 0225 310609/
310709
Fax: 0225 446675

Phillips – Bristol
71 Oakfield Road,
Bristol, Avon BS8 2BE
Tel: 0272 734052

Phillips – Cardiff
9–10 Westgate Street,
Cardiff,
Glamorgan CF1 1DA
Tel: 0222 396453

Phillips – Chester
New House,
150 Christleton Road,
Chester,
Cheshire CH3 5TD
Tel: 0244 313936/7

Phillips – Chichester
Baffins Hall,
Baffins Lane,
Chichester,
West Sussex PO19 1UA
Tel: 0243 787548

Phillips – Colwyn Bay
9 Conwy Road,
Colwyn Bay,
Clwyd LL29 7AF
Tel: 0492 533406

Phillips – Cornwall
Cornubia Hall,
Eastcliffe Road Par,
Cornwall PL24 2AQ
Tel: 0726 81 4047/8/9
Fax: 0726 817979

Phillips – Exeter
Alphin Brook Road,
Exeter, Devon EX2 8HT
Tel: 0392 439025
Fax: 0392 410361

Phillips – Guildford
Millmead,
Guildford,
Surrey GU2 5BE
Tel: 0483 504030

Phillips – Folkestone
11 Bayle Parade,
Folkestone,
Kent CT20 1SQ
Tel: 0303 45555

Phillips – Ipswich
Dover House,
Wolsey Street,
Ipswich IP1 1UD
Tel: 0473 255137

21 St. Peter's Street,
Ipswich
Suffolk IP1 1FX
Tel: 0473 254664

Phillips – Knowle
The Old House,
Station Road,
Knowle, Solihull,
West Midlands B93 0HT
Tel: 0564 776151

Phillips – Leeds
17a East Parade,
Leeds, West Yorkshire
LS1 2BU
Tel: 0532 448011

Phillips – Manchester
Trinity House,
114 Northenden Road,
Sale,
Manchester M33 3HD
Tel: 061 962 9237

Phillips – Morley
20 Fountain Street,
Morley, Leeds
LS27 9EN
Tel: 0532 523888

Phillips – Newport
(I.o.W.)
Cross Street,
Newport,
Isle of Wight PO30 1PT
Tel: 0983 822031

Phillips – Oxford
39 Park End Street,
Oxford OX1 1JD
Tel: 0865 723524
Fax: 0865 791064

Phillips – Plymouth
Armada Street,
North Hill,
Plymouth PL4 8LS
Tel: 0752 673504

Phillips – Ringwood
54 Southampton Road,
Ringwood,
Hampshire BH24 1JD
Tel: 0425 473333

Phillips – Rye
Cinque Ports Street,
Rye,
East Sussex TN31 7AL
Tel: 0797 225090

Phillips – Scotland
65 George Street,
Edinburgh EH2 2JL
Tel: 031 225 2266
Fax: 031 220 2547

207 Bath Street,
Glasgow G2 4HD
Tel: 041 221 8377
Fax: 041 226 4441

Phillips – Sevenoaks
49 London Road,
Sevenoaks
Kent TN13 1UU
Tel: 0732 740310

Phillips – Sherborne
Long Street Salerooms,
Sherborne,
Dorset DT9 3BS
Tel: 0935 815271
Fax: 0935 816416

Phillips – St. Ives
(Cambs)
The Market,
Station Road,
St. Ives,
Cambridgeshire PE17 4JA
Tel: 0480 68144

Phillips – Sturminster
Newton
The Corn Exchange,
Market Place,
Sturminster Newton,
Dorset DT10 1AT
Tel: 0258 73543

Phillips – Weston-
Super-Mare
Station Road,
Weston-Super-Mare,
Avon BS23 1XU
Tel: 0934 633174

Phillips – Winchester
The Red House,
Hyde Street,
Winchester,
Hampshire
Tel: 0962 62515

Phillips – Wymondham
The Saleroom,
Station Road,
Wymondham,
Norfolk
Tel: 0953 602661

OFFICES

Phillips – Barnstaple
10 Taw Vale,
Barnstaple, North Devon
EX32 8NJ
Tel: 0271 74487

Phillips – Cambridge
The Golden Rose,
17 Emmanuel Road,
Cambridge CB1 1JW
Tel: 0223 66523

Phillips – Carlisle
48 Cecil Street,
Carlisle,
Cumbria CA1 1NT
Tel: 0228 42422

Phillips – Carmarthen
33 King Street,
Carmarthen, Dyfed
Tel: 0267 238231

Phillips – Darlington
26 Cockerton Green,
Darlington DL3 9EU
Tel: 0325 382324

Phillips – Market
Harborough
33a High Street,
Market Harborough,
Leicestershire,
LE16 7NL
Tel: 0858 410060

Phillips – Melbourne
1 Chapel Street,
Melbourne,
Derbyshire DE7 1EU
Tel: 0332 863761

Phillips – Norwich
Whitefriars House,
52 Fishergate,
Norwich,
Norfolk NR3 1SE
Tel: 0603 616426

Phillips – Rochdale
19 Drake Street,
Rochdale OL16 1RE
Tel: 0706 351004

Phillips – Wimborne
1 The Square,
Wimborne,
Dorset BH21 1NF
Tel: 0202 841081

REPRESENTATIVES

Channel Islands
Richard Whitford,
Al-Mal House,
Rue du Pre,
St. Peter Port,
Guernsey
Tel: 0481 22448

Ariel Whatmore,
Les Aix,
St. Peter, Jersey
Tel: 0534 64289

Eire
Donal O'Neil Flanagan
O'Neil Flanagan &
Partners,
25 Catherine Street,
Waterford, Eire
Tel: 353 513 2311

Mrs Christine Ryall,
The Old Rectory,
Timolin Moone,
County Kildare, Eire
Tel: 353 507 24130

Northern Ireland
Mrs A. J. Cramsie,
O'Harabrook,
Ballymoney,
County Antrim
Tel: 02656 65808

Isle of Man
John Walsh
Tel: 0706 351004

Somerset & E. Devon
Lt.Col. Tim Courtenay
Whitehall Manor Farm
Hemyock, Cullompton
Devon EX15 3UQ
Tel: 0823 680444

Introduction

MOST PEOPLE who embark on buying antiques know a little about the subject and, in general terms, what it is they want to buy: a piece of silver, a set of chairs, a clock, a desk or a piece of porcelain. They seldom set out at the beginning to become experts, collectors or buyers of more than one or two things. Maybe they have become householders for the first time, or they need to refurnish a room, or have a little money to spend on something which will give pleasure as well as appreciate in value over the years. In theory it seems a simple matter. But all too often they find the choice alarmingly large, alarmingly different in price and exceedingly hard to understand.

Legislation and consumer protection in recent years has in a way made life more difficult for the prospective buyer rather than more simple. Antiques are not an exact science, and descriptions in catalogues and on labels and tickets are necessarily vague because the law requires provable facts and in the world of antiques these are often few and far between. It is up to the buyer to ask the questions, which will be answered most willingly and helpfully and indeed are essential if misunderstandings are not to occur.

Obviously it is not possible within the compass of such a small book to include every piece of information, every price and every article. Shelves of books in libraries and great tomes of prices of objects which have passed through the salerooms testify to that fact. It is possible, however, to distil the basic facts about the whole complex field into an easily readable, understandable form, so that anyone venturing out into the world of antiques is equipped with a general idea of price, period, form and value. Armed with this knowledge they will neither feel ignorant nor foolish and, by knowing the right questions to ask, will be able to avoid the major mistakes and pitfalls of the market.

Where to start

This guide is not, in the sense that most guides are, solely a price guide, nor is it crammed with useful but unconnected pieces of information which may further confuse the buyer. The aim of this guide is to help the potential antique-buyer firstly to identify in general terms the different periods, styles and designs of furniture, silver, clocks, pottery, porcelain and glass. And secondly to give guidelines which can safely be followed concerning the current price trends.

Each section is set out in chronological order, so that changing styles can be seen in their proper progression. Names of the best-known makers, together with their dates, can be referred to quickly and easily. Different woods used in cabinet-making are listed, with the periods during which each was most commonly used. The various stages in the development of pottery through to 'porcelain' are shown with typical examples, together with an explanation of the precise difference between all the various 'bodies' from pottery to stoneware to soft-paste and hard-paste porcelain to bone china. The development of movements in clocks, both longcase, lantern and bracket is traced, with examples of all the various stages. The use and meaning of hallmarks on silver is explained, and the growth of the glass industry in England from the first use of 'lead glass' or 'flint glass' instead of Continental soda glass which it almost totally replaced. And there is a simple guide to the prices you may expect to pay, depending on condition, fluctuations in the market, and availability.

Catalogues of saleroom prices, either in London or in the provinces, are useful reference books, particularly for the trade, but to a beginner they may often be misleading. Saleroom prices everywhere are as difficult to predict as the English weather – and can produce equally baffling results. Quite often the prices realized depend as much on who attends the sale as on what is being sold. To give an example: on one day, a piece of porcelain may be the object of intense competition between two dealers or collectors, both prepared to pay almost anything to acquire it. Some time later at another saleroom, an almost identical object can sell for less than half the price, because the competition is not there. Somewhere in between those two extremes lies the price a good antique dealer will be asking.

To a certain extent that price will be affected by current trends in the salerooms and current fashions, both here and overseas. But many antique dealers buy privately, and from each other, for prices which are less influenced by the volatile figures achieved at auction. Which is not to say that buying at auction is to be discouraged for private buyers. There are still good things to be bought in the salerooms, and for reasonable prices, providing the newcomer is prepared to tread warily and keep a cool head.

How to buy

The golden rule for buying antiques of any sort is to buy what you really like. It is you who will have to live with it, use it, clean it, polish it and show it off. Today, as in clothes, taste and fashion are eclectic and there is little point in owning something which makes you feel uncomfortable, however expensive or trendy it may be. If a teapot won't pour, don't buy it, however famous the maker. If the clock is exceptionally beautiful but its chimes are going to drive you mad, buy one a little less beautiful but which you can silence when you feel like it. If you can't sit at a dining room table because the chairs are too low or too high, even though they cost a King's ransom they aren't worth the price.

Above all, keep a sense of proportion. Compare the cost of a new canteen of silver with an old one by mixed makers and remember that ultimately you are buying knives and forks as well as silver. What would a brand new dinner service cost compared to a part service of Coalport or Derby? Or a set of dining chairs from a fashionable department store?

Introduction

Strange things happen to people's sense of values sometimes, and the actual purpose of an article seems to get forgotten in the heat of the moment. They become obsessed with the thought that they may have 'paid too much' for something, quite forgetting that the same object would probably cost twice as much brand new, if it could be found at all.

What to know

Some words hold a wealth of meaning, both in the trade and in the salerooms. They are used as a kind of shorthand and are not intended to deceive anyone, but, as in any other private vocabulary, outsiders often misunderstand the words, and regrettable mistakes may follow. Here are some of the most common: "Period" means 'of about the same date' as in "Chippendale period". "Style" means 'after the style of' and usually means a later copy or reproduction, as in "Adam style". "Chippendale" these days is used, as it is in America, to denote a particular style rather than as a direct attribution to the workshop of the man himself. The same applies to "Sheraton" and "Hepplewhite". "Georgian" is often used to describe a certain style as well as the period itself, and even when used as a form of dating is very loose and can mean any date for more than a hundred years, from 1714 to 1820. The same applies to "Queen Anne" as a description of style rather than period, particularly in the case of silver. "Provincial" is perhaps a slightly derogatory term when used for furniture, but a 'provincial' longcase clock or bracket clock denotes one of a particular design. In silver, 'provincial' may mean an assay office outside London, often rare, collectable and thus more expensive. "Sheffield Plate" or "Old Sheffield" means plated silver made from *c*.1740 by a special process. It should not be confused with the hallmark of the Sheffield Assay Office, which was in operation from *c*.1773 and prolific during the Victorian and Edwardian periods.

The descriptions to all the illustrations contain most of the technical terms in current use. When in doubt, use the glossary.

Where to buy

Antique dealers

Almost without exception, all established dealers are well qualified in their particular field, helpful, friendly and co-operative. Their prices are probably slightly higher than those in the salerooms, but like any other retailers, they have to cover their overheads and running costs, as well as giving you the benefit of years of experience, judgement and specialist knowledge. If there is anything that puzzles you, be it about price, period or quality, do not hesitate to ask. One vital question in every field should be 'Has it been restored?' or 'Do you know if it has been repaired?' Many dealers rescue wrecks from total extinction and, with the services of a qualified craftsman have the pieces restored to all their former glory. In these days of conservation, there is nothing wrong at all about such a practice – quite the contrary. But the dealer should tell his customers that it has been done.

Some dealers may have a notice "Trade only" in their windows. Private customers thinking to outsmart the dealer may find themselves with problems – anyone pretending to be 'trade' may well lose their legal protection as a private buyer or consumer. An antique shop is not a bazaar, and dealers dislike people who try and bargain with them without knowing what they are talking about. It is perfectly permissible to ask if the dealer will come down a little in his price, and if you show genuine enthusiasm for a particular piece they may well bring the price down just a bit, particularly if the object in question has been part of their stock for some time. But don't count on it.

Make certain you have a proper receipt for your purchase, stating clearly the total price paid, including VAT if applicable, and a full description of the piece which has been sold to you. The receipt will safeguard you against any possible errors on the part of the dealer and, providing you have good reason, allow you to return the article in the case of any errors you yourself have made.

Fairs and markets

These are fascinating places for the treasure-seeker and bargain hunter. Prices are usually lower than anywhere else, since the dealers have virtually no overheads, but the customer has little or no redress against any of the 'tricks of the trade'. As in all markets, there is likely to be a fair complement of 'fly-by-nights' among the genuine regulars, and it is a mistake to buy anything in a hurry. If you are serious about buying, spend some time just walking about, discovering who the 'regulars' are and who is unknown to the other dealers. If you see something you like, ask for a card giving the name and address of the dealer before even considering parting with your money. Most one or two-day fairs are put on by fair organisers who hold lists of names and addresses of all the dealers. The organiser's name is to be found displayed on posters and advertisements announcing the fair. In an open market you are on your own. Everyone has stories about finding wonderful things and everyone has stories about being taken for a ride.

It must be added that both in fairs and regular antique markets there are many stallholders who are extremely reputable and run small antique dealing businesses from their homes, travelling around fairs to find new customers. Many of them are only too happy if you suggest visiting them at their own addresses to see the rest of their stock.

Salerooms

Compared with the number of people who have ventured into antique shops or strolled down street markets, few people have been to an auction of any sort. Whether it is for farm machinery or wine or wholesale fruit and vegetables, all auctions are exciting, heady and unpredictable. And every auction house has a set of conditions of sale, setting out quite clearly all the details of the auction house's responsibilities. It cannot be repeated too often that *a saleroom is only acting as an agent for the seller*, and is in no way responsible for the condition or authenticity of anything which passes through its hands. This disclaimer is to be found in the conditions of sale of every variety of auction, not just those of antiques. It is essential, therefore, that the potential buyer reads these conditions of sale very carefully, and every time a different saleroom is visited, because the conditions vary. Check whether a buyer's commission is charged – many provincial salerooms have followed the big London auction rooms and charge a percentage which is added to the 'hammer price' plus VAT.

Introduction

This varies, but it is usually between 8 per cent and 10 per cent. Payment must be made when stipulated – usually within 48 hours of the sale, and goods must be removed by the time stated – Phillips allow seven days, other auction houses may have a different time-limit. If the goods are not removed, the auctioneer has the right to resell them and charge you the costs of storage and the standard charges for selling the article.

Some salerooms simply print in their catalogues 'imperfections not stated', others that the absence of any description of damage does not imply that there are no defects and/or restoration. Frequently the only hint of poor condition or damage are the letters 'a.f.' meaning 'as found' and usually implying considerable damage. All Phillips' catalogues contain a short glossary of the code used in descriptions, and damage is usually fully described in the text, but they add that 'care is taken to ensure that any statement, e.g. as to maker, set number, description and condition is reliable and accurate, but all such statements are statements of opinion'.

All lots are available to be viewed before the sale – times of viewing are announced and printed in the catalogue. It is helpful when viewing to take into consideration the general standard and condition of everything else in the sale as well as the piece you may have your eye on. If the general standard is low and condition poor, look at your 'find' again. Read the descriptions carefully and check any coding for condition. There is a complete vocabulary for the description of antiques and if you do not understand any of the words, use the glossary at the back of this guide. It contains most of the words in current use in the categories the guide covers.

Estimates Where auction houses publish estimated prices, either at the end of each description in the catalogue or on a sheet displayed prominently on viewing day, check your price-limit against them, but remember that these are a guide only to the amount the saleroom expects it to fetch on the day of the sale.

Reserves Most salerooms, including Phillips, state that all goods are put up for sale without reserve unless written instructions are received from the seller. These days it is rare for anything of any value to be sold without a reserve however. This is the price that the seller is prepared to accept for an object. If the bidding does not reach this figure it will be marked 'unsold' or 'bought in' in the auctioneer's book, although the auctioneers reserve the right to sell after the auction by private treaty after consultation with the seller. If yours was the last bid, but was below the reserve, you may ask the auctioneer after the sale if the seller is willing to accept your figure. No reserves are disclosed but are a confidential matter between the seller and the auctioneer. Unsold lots are not disclosed until after the sale.

Commission bids If you doubt your own nerve and would prefer not to bid yourself, or if for some reason you have attended the viewing and cannot attend the sale, make yourself known to a member of the auction room staff who will bid on your behalf. This is known as a 'commission bid' and accounts for an auctioneer's behaviour when he raises the bidding when there is apparently no one in the saleroom making any bids. As a further signal, if the commission bid seems to be the highest,

Introduction

the auctioneer will usually say 'With me, then, at . . .' and name the bid. When instructing someone to bid on your behalf it is a good idea to leave a little to his discretion. Remembering that you must add 10 per cent to the 'hammer price' for buyer's premium with an additional 15% VAT charge of the premium, give him your top figure, for the sake of argument say £200 but allow a couple more bids at his discretion, taking the 'hammer price' to £210 or £220. He will use those extra bids only if he feels they will secure the article for you.

Periods, dates and styles

Even when they are not being used to denote a style rather than a period, such as "Georgian", "Queen Anne" or "Adam" the naming of a period after a monarch does not mean precisely the dates of that monarch's reign. Changes were not abrupt but slow, gradually evolving from one style to another. Thus "William & Mary" runs from roughly 1690 to 1700, although William of Orange came to the throne in 1688 and reigned alone after the death of the Queen in 1694 until 1702. In metals and in pottery, this period is particularly important however and is precise: "William & Mary" 1688–1694 and "Williamite" 1694–1702. Again, Queen Anne's reign was remarkably short, a brief twelve years from 1702 to 1714 but it was an important period in terms of English style and changes in lifestyle and can often refer to a period almost ten years later, before the German lifestyle of the Hanoverian Georges filtered through from the Court to the upper and middle echelons of society. On page 14-16 there is a simple chart showing the main influences in change of style, use of material and naming the periods appropriately for each subject – there are slight variations in different fields – which can be used as a quick reference.

Country and provincial
The term "country furniture" is a relatively recent one, and denotes furniture made by country craftsmen, often in less expensive, more readily available woods. It is more simply made, often using traditional methods of construction, but following the general lines of the important cabinet makers and furniture makers of the period. Some examples of "country furniture" can be found on pages 90-91.

"Provincial" means different things in different fields, but in furniture particularly, it denotes furniture made, often to patterns by Chippendale, Hepplewhite and so on, but in provincial workshops, which often lagged behind "London" fashion by twenty years or more. Provincially-made furniture is sometimes more ostentatious and heavier in style than "London" furniture because provincial workshops wished to impress their clients with their expertise, and because their clients in turn wished to impress the local gentry with their newly acquired wealth. Once power-driven machinery was introduced into furniture-making and it began to be mass-produced in the provinces as well as in London, the difference was often even more marked, but from c.1880 there were no "country" versions of such fashionable articles as sofa tables, chiffoniers, and so on because they were being made cheaply enough in furniture factories and required techniques which only machines could achieve. Country craftsmen continued, however, to make traditional furniture such as gate-legged tables, Windsor chairs, dressers, corner cupboards, chests, and functional articles of every kind from the same traditional materials that had been used for centuries. The same is true for all the subjects covered in the guide – the advent of machine-made techniques did not obliterate the local potter, silversmith, clockmaker, cabinet-maker or craftsman. Indeed, many local skills were revived with the Arts & Crafts Movement in the 19th century, and many traditional shapes and forms were mass-produced during the Victorian and Edwardian periods.

A final word of warning on these products of "Tudor" and "Elizabethan" revivals. Great quantities of them were made, and now come within the legal definition of 'antique' i.e. a hundred years old or more. Many of them were finely made, by individual craftsmen and have in recent years acquired a high market value. But many of them were poor quality, made cheaply for the mass-market and of questionable design. With a little time and experience in handling antiques of all kinds, the difference will become obvious. Meanwhile it is as well to remember those trade words mentioned on page 11 and if in doubt the question "Can you be more precise about the date it was made?" can prove invaluable.

PERIOD	FURNITURE	CLOCKS	SILVER	POTTERY & PORCELAIN	GLASS
1660 1660 Fire of London CAROLEAN Charles II 1660–85	OAK Christopher Wren Rebuilding of London 1666	1658 John Fromanteel Pendulum clocks London Longcase Clocks Verge Escapement Joseph Knibb 1640–1712	EARLY ENGLISH Dutch influence Christian Van Vianen d.1660	Tin Enamel Delft Fulham 1670	George Ravenscroft flint glass c.1670
1680	Chinoiserie Inlay		Chinoiserie	Blue & White Oriental	
James II 1685–8 WILLIAM & MARY 1658–94	OAK WALNUT marquetry, parquetry Veneer Daniel Marot	Thomas Tompion 1639–1713	1685 Revocation of the Edict of Nantes Huguenot immigrants Jean Berain 1638–1711 Britannia Standard 1697	White Saltglaze c.1684	
1700					
QUEEN ANNE 1702–14	Grinling Gibbons 1648–1721 William Kent 1683–1748	Anchor Escapement	QUEEN ANNE Paul de Lamerie 1688–1751 BAROQUE ROCOCO	Liverpool c.1710 Meissen hard-paste porcelain c.1710 1720	Methuen Treaty 1703 Port & Sherry 1713 German/Silesian glass imports Newcastle glass Engraved glass
1730	WALNUT MAHOGANY Provincial Longcase				
George I 1714–27	Thomas Chippendale 1718–79 William Vile d.1767		1740 Sheffield Plate	Bow 1745–75 Chelsea 1745–69	Stourbridge-Brierley Hill 1740 GLASS TAX 1745

14

Period	Furniture	Clocks	Silver	Pottery & Porcelain	Glass
				c.1750	Coloured glass Air-twists *c.1755* Opaque Air-twists
EARLY GEORGIAN George II 1727–60	Robert Adam 1728–1792 Gillows of Lancaster 1761–1906	Regulator clocks *c.1752*	Robert Hennell 1763–1813 Hester Bateman 1761–90 → CLASSICAL	Wedgwood creamware *c.1750* Worcester First Period *c.1755–83*	
1760					
George III 1760–1820				Plymouth *c.1770–1810* HARD-PASTE PORCELAIN *c.1768* Bristol hard-paste Porcelain *c.1770* Caughley *c.1775–99* SOAPSTONE PORCELAIN Wedgwood pearlware *c.1779* Masons ironstone *c.1792* Minton *c.1793* Spode bone china *c.1794* Derby bone china *c.1810*	Waterford glass houses established *c.1760* Cut glass chandeliers GLASS TAX DOUBLED 1776 Tax on enamelled glass *c.1777* English glassmakers to Ireland 1780 Nailsea glass 1788 Heavy Waterford glass
LATE GEORGIAN	George Hepplewhite d.1788 MAHOGANY → SATINWOOD → Thomas Shearer		Boulton & Fothergill 1773–1809 Henry Chawner 1786–1810		
1810			→ REGENCY		
1815 BATTLE OF TRAFALGAR	← Thomas Sheraton Thomas Hope 1770–1831 Brighton Pavilion 1817 Chinoiserie French Empire		← Paul Storr 1792–1838 Hunt & Roskell Rundell, Bridge, Rundell Brighton Pavilion 1817 Chinoiserie French Empire	Nantgarw Swansea 1813–20 Doulton *c.1815* Rockingham bone china *c.1825*	Graeco-Roman & classical Coloured glass Wall lights, chandeliers GLASS TAX–IRELAND 1825
George III 1760–1820 **REGENCY**					

Date / Period	Furniture & Design	Silver / Metalwork	Clocks / Time	Ceramics	Glass
George IV 1820–30	Baroque Revival c.1820 'Abbotsford' Tudor & Jacobean (Sir Walter Scott)	Baroque Revival Emes & Barnard 1829			American press-moulded glass imports c.1825
1830					
WILLIAM IV 1830–37	Gothic Revival Medieval & Romantic	Gothic Revival Electroplating 1840 Electrotyping Elkingtons 1843	Skeleton clocks	Chamberlain's Worcester 1840–52	English press-moulded at Stourbridge, Newcastle c.1833
Victoria 1837–1901 EARLY VICTORIAN	OAK REVIVAL				GLASS TAX LIFTED 1845 Iridescent glass Cameo glass
1851 Great Exhibition					
1860	William Morris 1834–96	Arts & Crafts Movement Japonaiserie		Royal Worcester 1862 Belleek 1863	
	Arts & Crafts Movement Edward Ashbee 1863–1942	ART NOUVEAU Acid Engraving, Acid etching c.1870		ART NOUVEAU Lambeth Doulton Hannah Barlow	ART NOUVEAU Acid etching, engraving 1870 Gallé 1846–1904 Daum 1853–1909 Thomas Webb Queens Burmese ware 1885
LATE VICTORIAN Victoria 1837–1901	ART NOUVEAU E.W. Godwin 1833–86 Liberty & Co. 1875 C.F.A. Voysey 1857–1941		1880 Greenwich Meantime		
1900					
Edward VII 1901–10 George V 1910–36	C.R. Mackintosh 1868–1928 'Glasgow School'			Martinware 1873–1915 William Moorcroft Macintyre 1897–1913	Aesthetic Movement Lalique 1860–1945 Tiffany 1848–1933
1914 EDWARDIAN First World War					
1918					

Furniture

Periods and styles

The shape, form and construction of antique furniture depends to a very great extent on the woods from which it is made, who used it, and for what purpose. Living conditions changed with the centuries, and whereas in Medieval and Tudor days there was very little furniture of any sort in all but the grandest houses, by the mid-18th century England had a prosperous middle-class living in well-built brick houses and the amount of furniture, its purpose and variety had grown enormously. From then until Victorian times, when rooms were over-furnished and cluttered with all manner of objects, social developments once again separated the rich from the poor, the well-endowed from the impoverished dweller in industrial towns with barely a stick of furniture to call his own.

Oak

This was the principal timber used in England for making furniture until the Restoration of Charles II in 1660. It is coarse-grained, splits easily and restricts shape and construction as well as moving and shrinking with time and atmospheric conditions. Mortise and tenon joints, panelled construction, chip carving and heavy relief carving, and turning on a lathe straight across the grain were the most suitable for oak. Heavy iron nails and steel strap hinges together with the limited number of tools used in those early days result in the typical chests, court cupboards, stools, tables, chairs and benches of the period sometimes known as the Age of Oak.

Walnut

After the Great Fire of 1666 London was almost completely rebuilt and the new houses with their multiplicity of rooms demanded a different sort of furniture from the old-fashioned high walls and timbered buildings. Twist-turning, marquetry, veneer and the use of walnut came into England from the Netherlands, first with the return of Charles II and then with William of Orange. The use and appearance of furniture changed radically: occasional chairs, chests with drawers, writing furniture and small tables furnished the neat new brickbuilt town houses and soon became fashionable all over England. Walnut is close-grained and will take both tight twist-turning and crisp detailed carving, as well as being able to be cut as a veneer. Oak could be twist-turned too, but it was difficult to achieve with the slow manpowered lathes, except on fairly thick timber which made it wasteful except for table legs and similar more heavy applications.

17

Furniture

Veneer

Veneer is laid on a 'carcase' which is the completed piece of furniture made of cheaper wood, without decorative carving, beading or ornament. At first in England veneer was used on oak carcases but it was not satisfactory because of the movement of the timber which caused veneers to lift, as well as the coarse-grained nature of oak which did not provide a smooth enough surface, and soon deal, pine and softwood were substituted for carcases. Wonderful decorative effects were achieved with marquetry, parquetry and inlay, as well as the use of lacquer for grand cabinets and chests. At first panels were imported from the East and applied to carcases, but by the turn of the century English lacquer or 'japanning' had taken the place of foreign imports and 'chinoiserie' was in great demand. Beechwood was also used, either stained or painted, particularly for chairs, as well as some yew wood, cedar and elm for country furniture.

Mahogany

Soon architecture in England became influenced by classical Greek and Roman styles, first with William Kent, then the Palladian style, and finally by the Adams brothers. Furniture too took on architectural shapes, with pediments and cornices and 'double-heighted' bureaus, bureau bookcases and bureau cabinets to accord with the lofty size of rooms. The springy nature of walnut had enabled craftsmen to design and make a whole new range of furniture, particularly chairs and tables which had no need of stretchers between the legs to hold them firm, but which were based on the 'cabriole' leg cut from a single piece of timber and using the natural spring of the wood. When mahogany first came into England some time between 1720 and 1730 it was found to be an even more satisfactory wood for furniture-makers, both as a veneer and a solid timber. It was close-grained, immensely strong, and came in lengths and widths hitherto unknown due to the size and girth of the trees. Double-heighted furniture which had been made in two parts, could be made as a single unit because of the length and strength of mahogany. From Thomas Chippendale's vision of unity and concord in interior design grew the sleek classical lines of 18th-century furniture, making maximum use of beautiful undecorated surfaces in richly figured veneers. The carcases were also made in a cheaper mahogany, often called 'baywood' instead of pine and softwood.

Taste changed and Hepplewhite followed the fashion for lighter-coloured woods, a more delicate interpretation of classical themes, and less severe, more fluid lines. By the end of the 18th century, Sheraton in his turn had further lightened the lines of furniture, using cane, lattice, and tapering legs, as well as simulated bamboo and painted decoration, with an eye to the expanding market and the first large furniture manufacturers, many of whom made excellent use of his designs. Mass-produced brass screws, hinges and furniture fittings made it possible for all kinds of doors, lids, leaves and flaps to meet with minute hairline joins, giving the impression of sleek unbroken surfaces.

Machines

The Regency period was at once the apogee and turning point of some of the finest furniture made in England. But with the opulence and ostentation of a rich and successful nation, the pure classical forms were gradually adulterated. Brass inlay, brass marquetry, ormolu mounts and gilded wood embellished furniture of all kinds, and machines began to do the work of skilled craftsmen. When cut by hand, veneers are an eighth of an inch (30mm) thick or more. Machines could cut them paper-thin, to one sixteenth of an inch (15mm) or even less. Handcut dovetail joints were chunky and longtailed – machines cut them shorter, stubbier and with mechanical precision. Turning on high-speed power-driven lathes allowed more coarse-grained woods to be used for more elaborate shapes, always mechanically symmetrical. When the Victorians began with nostalgia to reproduce early Tudor and Jacobean designs, with twist-turning and chip carving, the twists all turned the same way, the shallow machine carving bit into the grain where no hand-held chisel could make an impression without the wood splitting along the grain.

To these technical advances there were added every known variation in style and design, from Gothic to Regency revival, often mixed together with very questionable results. The Arts & Crafts Movement and Art Nouveau, both products of a reaction against the tasteless clutter of Victorian interiors, did much to revive the genuine art of the craftsman in England and indeed had repercussions on interior design throughout Europe, and in America.

Principal woods used in furniture-making and their purposes

Woods have different characteristics as well as colours and grains. Early woodworkers used woods most suitable for their purposes, because the wood itself dictated how it could be worked and the speed of man-powered lathes limited the amount of turning, carving and cutting. Machine tools can cut, turn and shape timber regardless of the nature and grain of the wood. This is a fundamental clue to the authenticity of antique furniture. *Note:* Country furniture is always in solid wood and never veneered.

Solid woods
Ash chairs, chair legs, 17th and 18th century.
Beech chairs, particularly twist-turned, 17th and 18th century.
Birch chairs 17th to 19th century.
Cedar 16th to 19th century and as cabinet fittings 18th century.
Chestnut some English country, but mainly continental.
Coromandel small items, 19th century.
Deal, Pine carcase wood 17th and 18th century. Cheap domestic furniture 19th century.
Elm chair seats, Windsors, 16th to 19th century. With oak in country furniture.
Fruitwood (apple, pear, plum) Country furniture to 18th century.
Mahogany Hispaniola from c.1730, Honduras from *c.*1750 and as carcase wood 18th and 19th century, known as 'baywood'. African in 19th century.

Furniture

Maple underframes for chairs, 18th and 19th century.

Oak all periods, country, and as drawer linings and cabinet fittings 18th and 19th century. Unseasoned as carcase in some 19th century.

Padouk often Dutch or Continental, mid-18th and English 19th century.

Pine, Deal carcase wood 17th and 18th century. Domestic furniture 18th and 19th century.

Plane chairs, underframes, fly brackets, 18th and 19th century.

Rosewood as veneer from mid-18th century, solid in 19th century.

Satinwood as solid from *c*.1780, from 19th century as a veneer.

Teak rare before 19th century then quite popular.

Walnut rich brown native English, and French to 1720. Virginia 'red walnut' (unpolished) from late 17th century. Machine cut polished (black) and unpolished from *c*.1830.

Yew wood Highly prized. Country furniture, particularly hoops on Windsors 16th–19th century.

Principal veneers

Amboyna 18th and 19th century.

Birch or Satinbirch 19th century.

Burr Walnut (also burr elm etc. meaning the root) 17th and 18th century.

Chestnut some use as substitute for satinwood late 18th and 19th century.

Coromandel 19th century.

Harewood (stained sycamore) 18th century.

Kingwood 18th and 19th century.

Laburnum 18th and 19th century.

Mahogany Hispaniola to *c*.1750, San Domingo and Cuban from *c*.1750. All varieties 18th century.

Maple stained, 18th century, 'birds' eye' 19th century.

Olive oyster veneer, parquetry, 17th and early 18th century.

Partridge 18th and 19th century.

Plum up to late 17th century.

Rosewood as veneer late 18th century. Solid, 19th century.

Satinwood as solid from *c*.1780, from 19th century as veneer.

Sycamore stained, known as 'harewood'.

Tulipwood from *c*.1780.

Walnut native English and French from late 17th and early 18th century.

Yew wood parquetry in 17th century, veneer in 18th century.

Zebrawood late 18th century and some 19th century.

Stringing, inlay and crossbanding

Boxwood 16th to 18th century.

Coromandel late 18th century and early 19th century.

Ebony late 17th–19th century.

Holly late 16th–18th century.

Kingwood late 17th, 18th and 19th century.

Mahogany 18th and 19th century.

Olive 17th and early 18th century.

Satinwood late 18th century.

Tulipwood from *c*.1780.

Walnut late 17th century and early 18th century.

Yew wood 18th century.

Zebrawood late 18th century and early 19th century.

A Carolean decorated oak open armchair with cane panel back
and pierced scroll cresting. Pair £1000–£1500.

Furniture

Principal furniture designers and cabinet-makers

Adam, Robert 1728–92. Second and best-known son of William Adam, Scottish architect.

Ashbee, C.R. 1863–1942. Founded Guild & School of Handicrafts. 1888.

Chippendale, Thomas *c*.1718–79. *The Gentleman & Cabinet Maker's Directory* published first edition 1754.

Eastlake, C.L. 1836–1906. *Hints on Household Taste in Furniture* first published 1868.

Gibbons, Grinling 1648–1721. Wood carver and designer, worked with Christopher Wren.

Gillow, Richard 1734–1811. Son, Richard 1773–1849. Firm of Gillows established 1761–1906.

Godwin, E.W. 1833–86. Architect, designer, textile and wallpaper designer, strongly influenced by Japanese.

Hepplewhite, George *d*.1786. *Cabinet Maker & Upholsterers' Guide* published posthumously 1788.

Heal, Sir Ambrose 1872–1959. Furniture designer, founder of progressive furnishing store, greatly influenced by William Morris, Ernest Gimson, Arts & Crafts Movement.

Hope, Thomas 1770–1831. Seminal influence in grand Regency design.

Ince, William. In parnership with John Mayhew. *The Universal System of Household Furniture* by Ince & Mayhew published 1760.

Kent, William 1685–1748. Architect and interior designer.

Linnell, John. Upholsterer and cabinet-maker working from *c*.1761. *d*.1796.

Manwaring, Robert. Chair-maker and designer. *The Cabinet and Chair-Maker's Real Friend and Companion* published 1765.

Marot, Daniel 1662–1752. Early Continental influence on English furniture.

Mackintosh, Charles Rennie 1868–1928. Breakaway furniture designer from the Glasgow school influential in Art Nouveau.

Mayhew, John. See Ince.

Morris, William 1834–96. Founder of Arts & Crafts Movement and craftsman revival.

Seddon, George 1727–1801. Cabinet-maker, member of the Joiner's Company, and Master in 1795.

Shearer, Thomas. Cabinet-maker, artist of many plates in *Cabinet Maker's Book of Prices* published 1788.

Sheraton, Thomas. *Cabinet Maker and Upholsterers' Drawing Book* published in 1791–94. *Cabinet Dictionary* published 1803.

Vile, William. Partner with John Cobb and cabinet-maker to George III. *d*.1767.

Voysey, C.F.A. 1857–1941. Important designer of Art Nouveau furniture.

A 17th-century carved oak open armchair with lunette shaped toprail and interlaced foliate and gouged back with incised floral ornament of a later date, having shaped arm supports and solid seat, on baluster column uprights united by stretchers. £500–1000.

A 17th-century oak panel-back chair with scroll arms, arcaded frieze to seat and turned arm supports. £2000–3000.

A 19th-century oak 'Derbyshire' chair with arms terminating in grotesque heads and foliate carved decoration. Pairs: £1000–1500.

23

Charles II twist-turned chairs in walnut with caned back and seat and raised front rail. Set of 4: £2500–3500.

One of a set of eight oak Carolean-style open-arm chairs with turned pillar back supports, scroll carved legs and scroll arms.
Set of 8: £3000–4000.

Ornately carved high-backed chairs in the style of Daniel Marot with carved centre stretcher, scroll legs and hoof feet with stuffover seat.
Set of 6: £4000–6000.

Wing chairs

Charles II carved walnut high-backed chair with Braganza scroll arm supports, carved scrolling front legs and turned stretchers. £3000–4000.

Wing chair in William & Mary taste with walnut frame, turned stretchers and outward-curving arms with typically rigid Victorian lines. £800–1200.

Queen Anne wing chair with walnut frame, outward-curving back legs and pad feet with flowing lines and outward-curving generous arms. £6000–8000.

Wing chairs

George I wing chair with cabriole legs with carved scallop knee decoration and pad feet, flowing shape and outward-curving arms. £4000–6000.

Antique carved gilt and gesso wing armchair in the George I taste, with stuffover arched back and scroll arm side supports, having stuffover seat and cushion, on slender cabriole legs with foliate pendant and scale cabochon decorated knees, terminating in pointed pad feet. £800–1200.

Bergères

George IV mahogany
Bergère, the buttoned
back and sides with
overscrolled toprail
and lotus lappeted
arm terminals and
supports, the bowed
padded seat on
turned and ribbed
tapering legs.
£1000–1500.

George III tub chair in Bergère style with carved mahogany
frame edged with brass studs and tapered square legs.
£2500–3500.

Queen Anne walnut dining chair with heavy seat frieze, cabriole legs, pad feet and single back stretcher.
Set of 8: £15 000–20 000.

Queen Anne walnut dining chair with curved seat, turned stretchers and plain cabriole legs.
Set of 8: £20 000–30 000.

George I dining chair with square seat frame, shallow-carved decoration to knees of cabriole legs and plain stout stretchers.
Set of 6: £10 000–15 000.

George II plain mahogany dining chair with raised front stretcher, straight back splat and stuffover square seat.
Set of 6: £4000–6000.

George II mahogany dining chair with elaborately-carved
shell decoration to knees of cabriole legs, ball-and-claw feet
and decorative back splat. Set of 6: £15 000–20 000.

George II carved mahogany dining chair with ornate cabriole
legs, raised decorative crest rail and curved back with pierced
and carved back splat. Set of 8: £30 000–50 000.

Carved mahogany dining chair from the Chippendale period with ornately-carved cabriole legs, ball-and-claw feet and over-running upward-curving crest rail.
Set of 6: £10000–15000.

A 19th-century, carved mahogany, dining chair in the Chippendale taste with plain cabriole legs and pad feet with 'ribbon' style back.
Set of 8: £4000–6000.

George III mahogany elbow chair in the Chippendale manner with S-scroll arms, square chamfered legs and decorative back.
Pairs: £3000–4000.

George II carved mahogany chair in Chippendale style with Gothic vase back splat and plain chamfered legs.
Set of 6: £6000–8000.

George III arm chair in the Chinese taste with lattice back and
cane seat, plain chamfered legs and decorative spandrels.
Pairs: £6000–8000.

George III carved mahogany chair in the Chinese taste with
'pagoda' crest rail and plain chamfered legs.
Set of 4: £3000–4000.

Early lyre-backed chair with Chippendale characteristics, tapered square-sectioned legs on castors and S-scroll arms. Set of 4: £20 000–30 000.

Round-backed chair with serpentine curve to the front seat rail, outward-curving back legs and fluted tapered square-sectioned legs. Set of 6: £3000–4000.

'Fauteuils'

Directoire carved mahogany fauteuils with rectangular upholstered panel backs and stuffover bowed seats having rectangular arm supports with palmette and roundel ornament, on square tapered legs with bun feet. Pair: £2000–3000.

Regency open-armed chair in painted and gilded beechwood with square back, raised crest rail, curved arms and elegant turned tapered legs on peg feet. Pairs: £4000–6000.

George III elbow chair in the French taste with carved frieze rail and knees, curved front legs and French scroll feet. £3000–4000.

Shield back

George III mahogany chair of Hepplewhite shield-back design with dished seat, square tapering legs and plain stretchers. Set of 6: £3000–4000.

George III carved mahogany chair in Hepplewhite style with shield back, stuffover seat, tapering square-sectioned legs with peg feet and plain stretchers. Set of 4: £2000–3000.

Ornate version of the shield back, with downward-curving open arms, curvaceous back and turned tapering front legs. Set of 4: £8000–12000.

Early 19th-century ebonised chair of shield-back design with painted decoration, Prince of Wales feathers back, downward-curving arms, stuffover seat and square-sectioned tapering legs. Pair: £6000–8000.

George III chairs in Sheraton style with carved mahogany square back, stuffover seat and tapering reeded legs. Set of 6: £4000–6000.

Plain provincial chair in Sheraton style with stuffover seat, reeded decoration to back uprights and tapering square-sectioned reeded legs. Set of 6: £3000–4000.

Carved mahogany dining chair of simple design with swagged carved back, leather seat of broad proportions, square tapering legs and plain stretchers. Set of 6: £3000–4000.

Painted satinwood chair with peacocks' eye and floral decoration, oval caned panel-back, cane seat and turned and tapered front legs with peg feet. Pairs: £1000–1500.

'Windsor'

An early 19th-century
yew-wood and elm
Windsor Elbow chair
with pierced vase splat
and stick uprights.
£1200–1500.

A 19th-century yew-wood
Windsor elbow chair, the
arched back with pierced fret
vertical splats, having an elm
seat on ring turned legs.
£600–800.

Late 18th-century yew wood
and elm Windsor chair with
saddle seat, turned legs and
'cows' horn' stretcher.
£1000–1500.

Sabre leg

Regency mahogany dining chair with sabre leg, upholstered seat and rope-twist back. Set of 6: £3000–4000.

Regency carved mahogany dining chair with S-curved arm, carved scrolled sabre leg and scrolled crest rail. Pairs: £3000.

Above Matching single carved mahogany dining chair with scrolled sabre legs and foliate carving and scrolled crest rail. Set of 6: £4000–6000.

Right Regency mahogany dining chair with rosewood-panelled bar top rail, flush sides and sabre legs with drop-in seat. Set of 6: £4000–6000.

Left Plain balloon-back chair with upholstered seat and square seat frame, with turned and tapering front legs. Set of 6: £800–1200.

Above right A 19th-century mahogany dining chair with stuffover seat, reeded carving to back uprights and turned and tapering legs. Set of 6: £1500–2000.

Ebonized dining chair designed by Bruce Talbert and made by Gillows, bearing their stamp, with bobbin-turned back and reel-turned and carved front legs with taper-turned stretchers. Set of 8: £800–1200.

Dining chair in walnut with drop-in seat, square, chamfered legs and slightly curving back, designed by Ambrose Heal. Set of 6: £600–800.

Victorian armchairs

Victorian carved rosewood frame armchair, with a stuffover button down back, scroll arm supports and foliate apron, on cabriole legs with castors. £600–800.

Victorian carved walnut frame armchair, the upholstered button down back with padded arm scroll supports and bowed seat, on cabriole legs and castors. £700–900.

A 17th-century oak refectory table with turned legs, floor-level stretchers, two plank width, with minimal decoration on the frieze and small shaped spandrels. 7ft/2.10m long. £6000–8000.

Carved oak refectory table, the overhanging rectangular plank top with frieze carved with a repeated mirrored S motif, on six turned legs with quatrefoil ovals united by rectangular stretchers, parts 17th century. 7ft 9in/2.36m. £2000–3000.

Early Dutch oak draw-leaf table with bulb-shaped legs with low flat stretcher and grooved corner decoration to the frieze. £3000–4000.

Early 17th-century oak credence table with octagonal folding top, simple turned legs and solid pegged stretchers, with a gate support pivoting from the back. 29 in/74.8 cm. £1000–1500. If English: £3000–5000.

An 18th-century yew wood gate-legged table with central drawer in the frieze, baluster-turned decoration to the plain square legs, small bun feet, and simple shaped frieze. 6½ft/1.98m. Rare £10000–15000. In oak £3000–4000.

George III mahogany spider-legged table with fine reel and bobbin-turned legs, and two gate supports to either leaf. 3ft 6in/1.07m. £1000–1500.

Below Late 18th-century mahogany drop-leaf table with reeded tapering legs and peg feet with triple reeding to the table edge. 4 ft 1 in/1.25 m. £2000–3000.

George II drop-leaf table in fine-grained mahogany with plain pad feet and gently tapering legs. 4 ft 6 in/1.37m. £3000–4000.

43

Below George III oval snap-top table on pillar-and-claw support, with turned column, reeded legs and cast brass shoes and castors. 5½ ft/1.68 m long. £6000–8000.

George III mahogany twin pedestal dining table with ring-turned columnar supports and grooved curved legs with cast brass shoes and castors. 6 ft 10 in./2.08 m. 2-pillar £8000–12000.

Early Victorian mahogany dining table with six concentric leaves on pull-out supports with simulated bamboo stretchers and applied ornament above round bun feet. £20000–30000.

Above George III snap-top oval table with ring-turned tapering columnar support and reeded legs with cast brass shoes and castors. 6 ft/1.80 m long. £5000–8000.

45

Regency rosewood circular snap-top table, cross-banded in yew wood on pillar-and-claw support with cast brass paw feet and castors. 3 ft/91 cm. £4000–6000.

Regency rosewood snap-top circular supper table with cut brass inlay on central plinth terminating in four splayed feet with cast brass paw feet and castors. 3 ft/91 cm. £8000–12 000.

Regency kingwood breakfast table with snap top, cross-banded in satinwood with reeded edge on four slender pillars and plinth terminating in satinwood and ebony inlaid curving feet with cast brass paw feet and castors. 4 ft 2 in / 1.28 m. £5000–7000.

Regency rosewood snap-top breakfast table, inlaid with brass stringing on four slender columns and plinth terminating in scrolled curving legs and cast brass lion's mask feet and castors. 47 in / 120 cm. £4000–6000.

George III library table inset with brown leather on tapering square-sectioned legs, brass shoes and castors, with two drawers in the frieze matched by two dummy drawers on the opposite side. 4 ft 2 in/1.28 m. £5000–7000.

Regency mahogany writing table with pierced brass gallery, on turned and reeded tapering legs, peg feet, brass shoes and castors, with two frieze drawers with lion's mask and ring handles. 3 ft 6 in/1.07 m. £6000–8000.

Regency mahogany library table inset with green leather with Greek key banding, on turned and tapering legs, with three frieze drawers and dummy drawers alternating on the sides. 5 ft 10 in/1.77 m. £6000–8000.

Small-sized Regency writing table with concave central frieze drawer and two pairs of drawers on either side, plain wooden gallery and turned and reeded tapering legs. 3 ft 2 in/98 cm. £2000.

49

Drum

Small-sized Regency mahogany drum-top library table in rosewood, inset with leather and boxwood stringing, on turned column and tripod legs, with alternate drawers and dummy drawers in the frieze. 2 ft 10 in / 90 cm diameter. £6000–8000.

Below Regency mahogany drum-top library table with eight drawers in the frieze, inset with tooled leather and boxwood stringing, on pillar support and four splayed legs with brass shoes and castors. 4 ft 4 in / 1.32 m. £10 000–15 000.

Regency rent table in mahogany with tooled leather inset, and eight frieze drawers labelled alphabetically in the frieze, on central pillar support and four reeded splayed legs with brass shoes and castors. 3 ft 7 in/1.09 m. £10 000–15 000.

Sofa

Left Regency mahogany and satinwood sofa table with boxwood and ebony stringing with one drawer and one dummy drawer on either side, one fitted with easel writing flap. 4 ft 11 in/1.50 m. £8000–12 000.

Above Sofa table in rosewood and satinwood of Sheraton design, cross-banded in satin birch with two drawers and two dummy drawers in the frieze, on slender turned columns and splayed legs with brass shoes and castors. £8000–12 000.

Right Early 19th-century satinwood inlaid and decorated sofa table, the hinged top crossbanded in purple-heart and having rounded corners containing two drawers in the frieze with foliate sprays. 5 ft 9 in/ 1.76 m. £3000–4000.

Georgian satinwood and decorated card table of bowed and broken outline having a baize lined hinged top, the frieze with chinoiserie figures and interlaced ribband flowerhead decoration, on square tapered gaitered legs. 3 ft 2 in/97 cm. £1000–1500.

Mid-18th-century card and games table with flush drawer in the frieze, with shell decoration to the knees of the slender cabriole legs, tapering to hoofed feet. 3 ft/91.5 cm. £3000–4000.

George II card table in red walnut and mahogany with shell-carved knees to the bold cabriole legs, terminating in ball-and-claw feet, with one drawer in the frieze and recesses for counters on the playing surface. 2 ft 11 in/89 cm. £6000–8000.

Regency rosewood and brass marquetry card table with D-shaped hinged top and anthemion decoration to the frieze and base of rectangular beaded pillar, on curved splayed legs below a central plinth, terminating in brass paw feet and castors. 2 ft 7 in/78.5 cm. Pair: £10 000–15 000.

Below Victorian demilune games table veneered in burr walnut with carved acanthus-leaf base to pillar and vineleaf decoration to the scrolled curving legs. 3 ft/91.5 cm. £1200–1800.

Regency rosewood games table with hinged sliding top concealing a panel for chess, the drawer beneath inlaid for backgammon, on ring-turned column and reeded, hipped, splayed legs, with decorative brass shoes and castors. 2 ft/62 cm closed. £6000–8000.

53

George III mahogany drop-leaf games table, the rectangular hinged top with a reversible centre panel inlaid for chess and enclosing a backgammon board, fitted with a frieze drawer, on square tapered legs with brass cappings and castors. 2 ft 9 in/83 cm extended. £1800–2500.

Partridge and satinwood games table with central panel for chess sliding out to disclose a backgammon board, on fine tapered legs with cross-stretchers. 3 ft 2 in/97 cm. £4000.

George III silver table in the Chippendale manner with
Chinese lattice gallery and decorative frieze, on cluster column
legs with block feet and castors. 2 ft 5 in/73.5 cm. £8000–
12 000.

George III mahogany
dumb waiter on tripod
stand, the three tiers with
reeded moulded edging
and the central pillar
turned with swirling knop
decoration. £2000.

Regency plate and cutlery stand with spindle-turned gallery and ring-turned legs with brass shoes and castors. £3000–4000.

Early 19th-century set of four quartetto tables in amboyna with boxwood stringing on straight-turned legs. £4000–6000.

George III burr yew wood and satinwood Pembroke table cross-banded in tulipwood with single frieze drawer and square tapering legs. 2 ft 8 in/81.5 cm. £6000–8000.

George III harlequin Pembroke table with satinwood cross-banding and rising top with two dummy drawers to conceal the well, and two matching small drawers, on slender, tapering legs. £10000–15000.

George III mahogany Pembroke table inlaid with harewood with a satinwood centre panel with floral inlay, cross-banded in rosewood and inlaid with husks and foliage, opening to form an oval table. £8000–12000.

George III Pembroke table in sycamore veneer with mahogany cross-banding with an inlaid marquetry conch shell opening to form an oval table. £8000–12000.

George III satinwood demilune with inlaid husk and foliage and ebony stringing with decorative paterae on the frieze and inlaid, square tapering legs with block feet. £4000–6000.

Below George III satin birch and mahogany demilune table with scallop-edged cross-banding and boxwood stringing with sunray veneer on square tapering legs and collared feet. £3000–4000.

George III demilune side table in sycamore veneer with mahogany cross-banding and inlaid marquetry conch shell and slender tapering legs on block feet. 2 ft 8 in / 81.5 cm. £3000–4000.

One of a pair of early 19th-century papier-mâché and gilt heightened occasional tables, with a rectangular top, trefoil platform and scroll feet. Pair: £2000–3000.

A 19th-century satinwood and painted centre table with swags and flowerheads encircling a central panel depicting a muse or goddess, shaped frieze and curved legs with French scroll feet and a small circular undertier. £1500–2000.

William and Mary laburnum and walnut cabinet with oyster veneer and boxwood stringing, a cushion drawer below the cornice, the stand with one long frieze drawer and twist-turned legs with flat stretchers. The interior is fitted with small drawers 3 ft 2 in/96 cm wide. £6000–8000.

William and Mary chest on stand with quarter-veneered doors strung with boxwood, a cushion drawer below the cornice, the stand with a single frieze drawer and twist-turned legs with flat stretchers and bun feet. 3 ft 6 in/1.07 m wide. £6000–8000.

George I walnut secretaire cabinet in two parts, with seaweed-marquetry panels and fitted fallfront secretaire drawer, above two short and two long drawers, on plain small bun feet. 7 ft 6 in / 2.29 m high, 3 ft 2 in / 96.5 cm wide. £15 000–20 000.

George II burr walnut secretaire with concave lunette in the base drawer inlaid with radial sunburst, the panelled doors concealing fitted pigeonholes and drawers. 7 ft 8 in / 2.34 m high, 4 ft 1 in / 1.25 m wide. £10 000–15 000.

Bureau-cabinet

Queen Anne walnut bureau-cabinet with broken-arched pediment and arched mirrored doors concealing fitted drawers and pigeonholes, with one long dummy drawer concealing the inner well, above two short and two long drawers with brass mounts and handles, on plain bracket feet. 7 ft 8 in/2.34 m high, 3 ft 2 in/97 cm wide. £25 000–30 000.

Queen Anne walnut bureau-cabinet with undulating arched pediment and arched mirrored doors, the interior fitted with flights of small drawers and compartments, and below the slope front a well above four shallow drawers with drop handles, on bracket feet.
7 ft 6 in/2.07 m high,
3 ft 6 in/1.07 m wide.
£30 000–40 000.

Early 18th-century walnut veneered fronted and pine sided bureau cabinet, the upper part with moulded cornice, the sloping fall with a book ledge enclosing a graduated and fitted oak and walnut interior with pigeonholes, drawers, enclosed central cupboard with arched panel door and slide concealing a well, containing three long featherstrung drawers, on plinth base and bun feet (parts later). 3 ft 2 in/97 cm wide. £3000–5000.

Bureau-cabinet

Early 18th-century walnut bureau-cabinet with block-fronted doors concealing a fitted interior, above the slope front, with fluted columns on either side of three graduated drawers, on plain bun feet. 7 ft 2 in/2.18 m high, 3 ft 3 in/99 cm wide. £10000–15000.

An 18th-century walnut crossbanded and featherstrung bureau cabinet, the upper part with moulded arched cornice and fitted with adjustable shelves enclosed by a pair of arched bevelled mirror glazed panelled doors and fitted with a pair of candlesticks below, the sloping fall enclosing a fitted graduated interior with pigeonholes, drawers and bowed central enclosed cupboard, having a well with a slide below, containing two short and two long drawers, on bracket feet. 3 ft 2 in/98 cm wide, 7 ft 4 in/2.24 m high. £8000–12000.

Bureau-bookcase

Chippendale period bureau-bookcase in mahogany with broken pediment, glazed doors with astragal moulding in star pattern, with an interior well concealed by two dummy drawers above three long graduated drawers, on bracket feet.
7 ft 1 in/2.16 m high, 3 ft 3 in/99.5 cm wide.
£15 000–20 000.

George III secretaire bookcase in satinwood and tulipwood with boxwood and ebony stringing, with applied decoration to the broken swan-neck pediment, dentil cornice, glazed doors with astragal moulding, the fallfront concealed by two cockbeaded dummy drawers above three graduated drawers, with narrow shaped apron and splayed feet.
7 ft 4 in/2.23 m high, 3 ft 5 in/1.06 m wide.
£20 000–30 000.

Bureau-bookcase

George III mahogany secretaire bookcase with swan-necked pediment and Gothic glazing bars to the doors and fielded panel doors below the fallfront concealing document drawers, on bracket feet.
7 ft 1 in / 2.16 m high, 3 ft 5 in / 1.06 m wide.
£6000–8000.

Late 19th-century mahogany and satinwood cross-banded secretaire bookcase with geometrical glazing bars and three graduated drawers, on splayed bracket feet.
7 ft 2 in / 2.18 m high, 3 ft 4 in / 1.02 m wide.
£6000–8000.

George III mahogany secretaire cross-banded with tulipwood, with swan neck pediment and dentil cornice with Gothic glazing bars to the doors, and three graduated drawers below the fallfront, on ogee bracket feet.
6 ft 6 in / 1.98 m high, 3 ft / 91.5 cm wide.
£8000–12000.

Queen Anne walnut bureau, the slope front quarter-veneered and cross-banded, with fitted interior and interior well concealed by a dummy drawer flanked by pull-out supports or lopers, above three graduated drawers, on bracket feet. 3 ft 3 in/99 cm high, 3 ft/91.5 cm wide. £6000–8000.

William and Mary oak bureau with split mouldings, the sloping fall with a book ledge enclosing a fitted graduated interior with drawers of concave outline, pigeonholes and well with sliding compartment with wrought iron clasp containing two short and two long drawers, on bracket feet. £2500–3000.

George III mahogany bureau with boxwood stringing and an interior well flanked by pull-out supports above two short and two long graduated drawers, on bracket feet. 3 ft 2 in/97 cm high, 3 ft 1 in/94 cm wide. £2000–3000.

George III mahogany bureau with brass mounted bail handles and escutcheons, the interior well concealed by a single dummy drawer above a flight of three graduated drawers, on carved ogee bracket feet. 3 ft 3 in/99.5 cm high, 3 ft/91.5 cm wide. £3000–4000.

George III mahogany architects' table with boxwood stringing
and double-ratcheted hinged top inset with leather, with three
frieze drawers matched by three dummy drawers on the
opposite side. 3 ft/91.5 cm wide. £4000–6000.

George III partners' pedestal desk in mahogany with tooled
leather-inset top, three drawers of equal width in the frieze,
and two flights of three graduated drawers on either side.
5 ft 2 in/1.57 m wide. £10 000–15 000.

Architects', partners' & pedestal

A 19th-century partners' desk with rounded corners on flush pedestal base and reeded edge to the leather-inset top, with three drawers of equal width in the frieze and two flights of graduated drawers on either side, fitted with Bramah locks. £6000–8000.

Below A 19th-century mahogany partners' pedestal desk with turned wooden handles, thumb-moulded edge to the leather-inset top, and two doors below concealing document drawers. £4000–6000.

Davenport

Victorian walnut Harlequin davenport with galleried rising compartment, with three central drawers between pigeonholes, the writing compartment with hinged ogee lid containing two drawers and an adjustable slope, with a bank of four drawers to one side, the front with floral carved scroll supports on castors. 1 ft 11 in/58 cm. £1800–2200.

Victorian davenport in walnut, cross-banded with thuyawood and with boxwood stringing, the top with pierced brass gallery, pull-out fitted writing drawer and four drawers in the base concealed by a flush-fitting door. 3 ft/91.5 cm high, 1 ft 9 in/53.5 cm wide. £2500–3500.

A 19th-century, small-sized, roll-top or tambour-topped ladies' writing table, with fitted interior and fitted writing drawer in the frieze, on square tapering legs and castors. 3 ft 1 in/94 cm wide. £4000–6000.

Late 19th-century kingwood and parquetry desk with gilt mounts and ornate gilt metal candleholders, in the manner of a small Carlton House desk, with curved fitted drawers, leather-topped writing surface and two drawers in the frieze, on curved tapering legs with gilt metal acanthus and paw feet. 3 ft 5 in/1.04 m wide. £3500–5000.

Late Georgian satinwood and tulipwood cross-banded cheveret with oval mahogany-veneered panels to two small doors concealing drawers and pigeonholes, with hinged baize-lined writing surface above a single flush-fitting frieze drawer. £4000–6000.

George III mahogany bonheur du jour or ladies' work table with undulating curved superstructure, the three central drawers flanked by flush-fitting doors concealing drawers, with hinged baize-lined writing top on square tapering legs and peg feet. £3000–4000.

Late Georgian satinwood and tulipwood bonheur du jour with swan neck pediment, inlaid chequerwork and small decorative medallions, on square tapering gaitered legs. £4000–6000.

George III mahogany cheveret with simple lines, hinged baize-lined writing surface with two pull-out supports, with turned bone handles, on square tapering legs. £3000–4000.

73

A 16th-century oak coffer of frame and panel construction
with coffered panelled lid with iron hinges and fastening, iron
carrying-handles and simple geometric carving on the front
panels. 4 ft 9 in/1.44 m wide. £3000–4000.

Early 18th-century coffer of panelled construction with a
hinged top, the front with stipple frieze decorated with foliate
meandering relief ornament with initials ML and dated 1780,
on moulded rectangular supports. 3 ft 11 in/1.20 m.
£600–800.

Massive Victorian stained-oak coffer of a type similar to Italian
'*cassone*' with mock-Tudor relief decoration and romantic
medieval figures, with lion's mask carving and brass ring
handles. £1500–2000.

74

A 15th-century aumbry or livery cupboard, often no more than oak doors set in the wall, with pierced Gothic decoration, iron cockshead hinges, probably made up later as a cupboard. £3000–5000.

Late 16th-century carved oak court cupboard with stylised tulip and scroll strapwork, reel-turned columns and guilloche frieze. £3000–4000.

75

Late 17th-century oak side table with turned wooden handles to the frieze drawer, thumb-moulded edging to tabletop, on reel-and-bobbin turned legs with plain square stretchers on small bun feet. 2 ft 8 in/81 cm wide. £1500–2000.

George II side table or low '*bois*' with a single drawer in the frieze, small shaped apron and fretted spandrels on four straight chamfered legs. 2 ft 10 in/86 cm wide. £1000–1500.

A 19th-century Dutch mahogany and floral marquetry lowboy
of arc en arbellette outline, the top with a vase of flowers,
birds, butterflies and scrolls, containing two long drawers,
on foliate carved cabriole legs with claw and ball feet.
2 ft 6 in/76 cm. £1500–2000.

George I walnut lowboy with moulded edge to top, projecting
drawer mouldings, brass backplates and simple bail handles,
with shaped frieze and nicely-shaped tapering cabriole legs
with pad feet. 2 ft 6 in/76 cm wide. £6000–8000.

Early 18th-century oak and elm lowboy with an overhanging oak top, containing a short and two deep drawers in the arched apron, on cabriole legs terminating in pad feet (some re-veneers and minor replacements). 2 ft 10 in/85 cm. £1200–1800.

An early 18th-century walnut and featherstrung lowboy, with a crossbanded top and a moulded edge containing three drawers in the arched apron, on cabriole legs with scrolls and pad feet. £2500–3000.

George I walnut kneehole dressing chest or writing chest, cross-banded with projecting lip moulding to drawers, plain brass backplates to simple bail handles, on neat bracket feet. 2 ft 7 in/79 cm wide. £6000–8000.

Early George III mahogany kneehole desk, with a moulded edge fitted with a slide, containing a long frieze, arched apron and six short drawers about a central enclosed cupboard flanked by fluted canted angles, on bracket feet. 2 ft 10 in/ 87 cm. £2000–3000.

Flat-fronted chests of drawers

William and Mary burr walnut chest of drawers with decorative feather stringing and narrow cornice below the cross-banded top, the sides also cross-banded, with plinth-moulded base on bun feet. 3 ft 2 in/96.5 cm wide. £5000.

William and Mary flat-fronted chest of drawers in oyster veneer and boxwood stringing with narrow cornice below the cross-banded top, the brass backplates of later date. 3 ft 2 in/96.5 cm wide. £6000–8000.

Flat-fronted chests of drawers

William and Mary walnut and marquetry flat-fronted chest of drawers with cross-banding and half-round moulding edging the carcase surrounding the drawers, on shaped bracket feet. 3 ft 1 in/94 cm wide. £6000–8000.

Queen Anne walnut chest of drawers with quarter-veneered top, the projecting drawer mouldings cross-banded. A shallow top drawer above three small drawers, a pair and two long graduated drawers with brass backplates and plain bail handles. Carrying-handles on either side. Plinth-moulded base and shaped bracket feet. 3 ft 1 in/94 cm wide. £15 000–20 000.

Queen Anne walnut bachelors' chest, feather-banded with hinged top supported on pull-out slides flanking two small drawers above three graduated drawers, on plinth-moulded base with plain bracket feet. 2 ft 4 in / 71.5 cm wide. £10 000–15 000.

George II mahogany chest with moulded edge to top and brushing slide and four graduated drawers, with gilt metal rococo backplates, handles and escutcheons, on plinth-moulded base with plain bracket feet. 3 ft 3 in / 99 cm wide. £3000–4000.

Late 17th-century oak clothes press with fielded panel doors fitted with shelves above, and drawers in the base with plain turned wooden handles, the base with curved bracket feet. 5 ft / 1.52 m wide. £1500–2000.

Queen Anne walnut chest on chest in fine cartouche veneered panels with boxwood and ebony stringing, cross-banded, with lip moulding to the edges and cornice, a cushion drawer below the cornice and the interior fitted with 11 shallow drawers and a secret drawer, on plain bun feet. 3 ft 5 in / 1.04 m wide. £6000–8000.

George I walnut tallboy made in two parts, with cross-banding to the projecting moulding round the drawers and half-round moulding between, with three small drawers at the top and graduated drawers in both halves, on plinth-moulded base with plain bracket feet.
3 ft 5 in / 1.04 m wide.
£6000–8000.

Ebonised oak wardrobe from the 'Arts & Crafts' movement of furniture design, after the style of the Glasgow school of C.R. Mackintosh with inlaid oval panels and stringing and a deep drawer in the base, on plain turned bun feet.
£1500–2500.

A 19th-century mahogany linen press or 'housekeeper's cupboard' with plain panelled doors and a secretaire drawer below flanked by two small drawers with three long graduated drawers below, with shaped apron and splayed bracket feet. £3000–4000.

A Victorian oak linen press with dentil cornice and arched moulding with leaf-carved surrounds to applied carved mythical beasts and scenes from mythology, and two full-length deep drawers in the base. £2000–3000.

Bow-fronted mahogany chest of drawers cross-banded in
satinwood with ebony and boxwood stringing of Sheraton
design, with fitted writing drawer above three full-length
drawers, on square tapering peg feet with cast brass shoes.
2 ft 10 in/86.5 cm high, 2 ft 11 in/89 cm wide. £3000–5000.

George III satinwood and burr yew wood demilune commode
with harewood, stained sycamore and palisander veneer
decorating the top wtih four graduated drawers on plain
square tapering gaitered feet. £10 000–15 000.

George II mahogany serpentine chest with canted corners, with gilt metal rococo handles and escutcheons, on plinth-moulded base with canted bracket feet. 3 ft 8 in/1.12 m wide. £10 000–15 000.

George III serpentine-fronted chest in mahogany, the drawer fronts cross-banded to simulate pairs of drawers, with cross-banded canted corners, on plinth-moulded base with canted bracket feet. 3 ft 2 in/96.5 cm wide. £8000–12 000.

George III satinwood and partridgewood dressing chest with fitted top drawer and oval veneered panel decorating the top, with slender canted corners on ogee bracket feet. £10000–15000.

George III mahogany serpentine-fronted dressing chest with cockbead surround to three graduated drawers with curved shaped apron on slender splayed feet. £5000–7000.

George III mahogany serpentine-fronted gentleman's commode with rounded corners and gilt brass rococo handles and escutcheons with crisply-carved flowerhead and foliate apron and foliate carving to the curved, scrolled legs and feet. £30 000–40 000.

A 19th-century marquetry and ormolu bombé commode in the French taste with marble top, inlaid with flowers, leaves and ribbons with shaped apron and outward-curving tapering legs with cast gilt metal scroll feet. £3000–5000.

89

Early 18th-century oak dresser base with plinth-moulded top and three drawers in the frieze, two in the curved, shaped apron, with two-plank potboard below and plain straight legs and feet. £4000–6000.

An 18th-century dresser in oak in North Country style with plank back to shelves and shaped uprights with a central flight of four drawers, flanked by cupboards with drawers above, on shaped bracket feet. £4000–6000.

A 19th-century corner cupboard with dentil moulding and serpentine-shaped base, with glazed doors and plank back, in stained pine with brass hinges and key-plate. £600–800.

Late 18th-century oak dresser base with pierced decorative scrolled apron and three drawers, on plain straight chamfered legs. 5 ft 10 in / 1.77 m wide. £4000–6000.

Late 18th-century full-length oak corner cupboard with plank back and glazed doors above two plain panelled doors in the base. £2000–3000.

George III mahogany secretaire bookcase with centre fall in the breakfronted base with geometric astragal moulding to the glazed doors and fitted with adjustable shelves. 8 ft 11 in / 2.72 m high, 4 ft 10 in / 1.47 m wide. £15 000–25 000.

Regency mahogany secretaire bookcase with applied decorative moulding and brass lattice grilles and pleated silk panels to the cupboards in the base. £8000–12 000.

Late Regency carved mahogany and ebony strung library bookcase in the manner of George Oakley, the upper part with a foliate scroll decorated pediment and cornice (one scroll missing), enclosed by four honeycomb trellis brass grille glazed panel doors with fluted fan spandrels between anthemion capital stiles, the lower part of broken outline enclosed by panel door of similar design, on carved paw ebonised scroll feet and plinth base. 7 ft 1 in/2.15 m wide. £10 000–15 000.

A 19th-century satinwood and marquetry breakfront library bookcase with central broken pediment and arched glazing bars, the doors inlaid and outlined in tulipwood and fitted inside with trays and shelves. 8 ft 9 in / 2.66 m high, 8 ft 4 in/2.54 m wide. £15 000–25 000.

Victorian oak library bookcase in high Gothic style decorated with gargoyles and winged cherubs and fantastic masks with carved scenes of bucolic country life on the base cupboard doors. £2000–3000.

George III mahogany serpentine sideboard, cross-banded in
tulipwood with boxwood stringing with single drawer in the
centre, flanked by a cellarette drawer and a cupboard, on plain
square tapering legs with spade feet. 4 ft 6 in/1.37 m wide.
£5000–7000.

George III serpentine sideboard in mahogany and satinwood,
inlaid with husks and decorated in the neo-classical taste, with
two drawers in the centre flanked by a cellarette drawer and a
cupboard, on square tapering legs with spade feet.
£6000–8000.

George III mahogany and boxwood strung bowfront sideboard with a crossbanded top, containing two central drawers flanked by a deep drawer to either side, on reeded tapered legs terminating in small feet. 4 ft/1.22 m wide. £2000–3000.

George III mahogany bow-fronted secretaire-sideboard with fitted secretaire drawer in the centre flanked by two deep drawers with cupboards below, with boxwood stringing to the door and drawer fronts and with slender decorative columns and reeded edge to the top. 3 ft 1 in/94 cm high, 5 ft 5 in/1.65 m wide. £3000–4000.

CHIFFONIERS

A 19th-century rosewood and brass inlaid chiffonier, the recessed superstructure fitted with three drawers, the lower part decorated with trailing husks and foliate stems and enclosed by a pair of arched panel doors, on sabre feet. 2 ft 6 in/75 cm. £1000–1500.

Regency carved rosewood side cabinet or chiffonier with acanthus leaf decoration to the scrolled uprights and pierced brass gallery inlaid with cut brass and with carved and gilded edging to the top and base, with cupboards below flanked by two decorative columns on carved turned feet. £6000–8000.

Regency rosewood and parcel gilt chiffonier with marble top, the sides supported with applied columns in the Egyptian style, with hinged fallfront above two brass lattice grille doors with pleated silk behind. £4000–6000.

Clocks

Few serious clock collectors are totally ignorant about the mechanism and movements of at least one kind of clock. Many people have begun collecting clocks as a result of being given or inheriting a clock of some description which may no longer be in working order. By tinkering about with it they eventually become totally absorbed in the mechanics of clockwork until it becomes a gathering passion. The actual movement of a clock, however, is only one factor which determines the value and rarity of an antique clock. The case-work and the shape and style of dial and hands also help to determine whether a clock is genuine or not.

At first glance, the prices paid for clocks seem to have no rhyme or reason: one clock sells for thousands of pounds while another, to all intents and purpose looking to the uninitiated almost the same, will fetch only a few hundred. It must be appreciated, first and foremost, that every clock of any age has been genuinely repaired in the course of its working life, and much depends on the quality and craftsmanship of those repairs. Many have had their movements altered or completely replaced, others have been codged up at some later date, or put together from bits of another clock of a similar period.

Essential facts

Since the earliest clocks with spring drive and fusee movement are outside the scope of this guide, progress is charted from the beginning of pendulum clocks, first invented in about 1658 and generally credited to John Fromanteel, though there are many other contenders for its origins. Without going into too many technical details, it is essential to know that early pendulum clocks had one hand only, a narrow chapter ring, and were marked with hours and half-hours only. From c.1690 the accuracy of the pendulum beat was such that in addition to hours, half-hours and quarters marked on the inside of the chapter ring in Roman numerals, a subsidiary seconds dial was added, marked in Arabic numerals. After this, a minute hand and markings for minutes were added to the outside of the chapter ring, once a longer pendulum replaced the short 'bob pendulum' of early lantern clocks. An intermediate stage, involving a pendulum with a wider swing, produced the 'wing clock'.

Longcase clocks developed in parallel with bracket clocks, both with pendulums but with slightly different movements. The longcase clock allowed for a longer period of going, and early London-made clocks, from c.1660, were almost all 8-day going, with two hands and subsidiary seconds dials. 30-hour clocks continued for some time to be made with one hand only, and only quarters marked on chapter rings. 8-day clocks were key-wound, whereas 30-hour clocks were wound by pulling down the endless cord with its various weights and counter-weights.

London and provincial

While London clocks were almost all key-wound 8-day going, provincial clocks were predominantly 30-hour going, which were far cheaper to make. Many provincial makers resorted to a simple deception by giving their clocks dials with winding holes, thus giving the illusion that the clock was an expensive 8-day going clock. Many honest provincial longcase clocks with 30-hour movements were made with one hand only, at least up to *c.*1740. So many, in fact as to indicate a preference rather than a limitation. Large numbers of these simple clocks have been altered at a later date, usually by replacing the 30-hour movement with an 8-day one, with two hands. Often, however, the dial has not been replaced, and a chapter ring with no minute markings quickly betrays this later modification.

The movement of a 30-hour clock was usually of birdcage construction, with upright posts or pillars holding the top and bottom plates together, in essence very similar to the construction of a lantern clock movement. In some cases the posts or pillars were often of fine-quality brass with decorative turning, and many of these have been removed from their provincial cases and converted into 'genuine lantern clocks' particularly during the Victorian period, when spurious signatures of such famous makers as Tompion or Knibb were added.

The movement of an 8-day clock is usually of plate frame construction, where the plates are set at the back and front as opposed to top and bottom, with shorter pillars or posts to hold them together. Where a 30-hour movement has been replaced by an 8-day movement, the shape of the case and dial will help to identify the modification, as well as holes in the plates and the 'seat board' on which the movement rests.

Case work

It will be realized that dial, movement and case must be in accord if the clock is authentic. Brass dials may have been substituted for later plain white dials – in some cases, arched dials have been put into a clock and the whole hood and case has been altered to accommodate them. As a general rule, cases follow the same periods and styles as those of furniture, certainly for London-made clocks, and a time-lag of as much as 20 years may occur between fashionable designs in London and the provinces. Early London longcase clocks were ebonised, either with ebony veneer on an oak carcase, or with stained pear wood, or in ebonised oak. It seems that early veneers and marquetry were laid on oak carcases for a longer period than furniture, which was generally made with a pine carcase from the late 17th century onwards.

Provincial longcase clocks were not made in any quantity much before *c.*1730, and were either in plain oak or in mahogany veneer, since the timber was shipped into Liverpool and was readily available. Although their styles may lag behind London clocks, provincial clocks were seldom of the plain, small, architectural designs of early London clocks. Their designs more or less coincide with the change from square-faced dials to arched dials.

On London longcase clocks, the arch of the dial was often simply decorative, or displayed the name of the maker, or was used for the strike/silent dial. In the provinces the arch was often filled with a lunar dial, and in London, Liverpool and other port towns there might be a tidal dial for high and low water, but these are more rare than moon phase dials. Automata were very fashionable from about *c.*1720 and the same rocking mechanism which drove the lunar dial was employed to drive all manner of little clockwork scenes.

Bracket clocks and carriage clocks

The development of bracket clocks follows slightly different lines in terms of movement, though the design of cases runs parallel to those of longcase clocks. The driving power was supplied by a spring enclosed in a drum. When the drum was turned with a key, a gut or chain was wound round a metal cone with a spiral track known as the fusee, which regulated the speed of the drive. Instead of a striking mechanism, many bracket clocks had a 'pull repeat' which, when a cord was pulled, repeated the stroke of the last quarter or half hour, depending on the mechanism. Backplates of bracket clocks are visible through the glass panels of the case, and were beautifully engraved with flowers, leaves, and often a cartouche enclosing the maker's name. From about 1720 onwards, the size of bracket clocks increased and many were made with anchor escapements instead of the original verge so far used in association with the fusee.

The miniaturized version of the bracket clock, the carriage clock, was originally the sole province of French clockmakers who equipped these little clocks – the mignonette was only about 4½in/11.4cm high – with chimes known as the 'petite sonnerie' or 'grande sonnerie', often combined with minute repeaters and even alarm mechanisms. A simpler version of this complicated and expensive mechanism was first produced by French maker Paul Garnier in the first half of the 19th century and this cheaper version of the 'pendule de voyage' proved extremely popular in England, where many of them were made by well-known London makers.

Regulators, skeletons and Acts of Parliament

Until 1752, time in England was reckoned by 'sundial' time, regulated to a certain extent by leap years. Sidereal time, equal to 365 days 6 hours 9 minutes, was adopted in 1752, and the regulating of time became an important factor to clockmakers, although it still varied by a matter of minutes from east to west, north to south. The simplest, most accurate of mechanisms were devised, called 'regulator clocks' which were essentially functional and stripped of all decoration. Early regulator clocks, with mercury-filled pendulums and mirrored backboards, are extremely attractive though later ones tend to be more functional and less pleasing. They might be said to be the forerunners of the skeleton clock, though the design of these is usually attributed to French clockmakers. Skeleton clocks first appeared in England in the mid-19th century, and many of them are of wonderfully Gothic design. Out of fashion for many years, they are now a growing collectors' market.

One curious oddity is the naming of wall-mounted tavern

clocks 'Act of Parliament' clocks. Such clocks were well-known long before a tax on clocks and watches was imposed in 1797, when the populace is supposed to have hidden their own clocks and watches to avoid paying tax and relied instead on large wall-mounted clocks in taverns and other public places. Certainly the Act had nothing to do with the 'Definition of Time' Act which came into force in 1880 when Greenwich mean time was accepted by all regions with the exception of Ireland which maintained Dublin time until 1917.

Notable clockmakers

London

Bradley, Langley. Clockmakers' company member from 1695–1738. Longcase and bracket, turret clocks.

East, Edward. Born 1602. Died 1696. Famous for clocks and watches. Chief Clockmaker to the King 1660.

Ebsworth, John. Clockmakers' company freeman 1665–99. Lantern, longcase, bracket clocks and watches.

Fromanteel, Ahasuerus 1. Born 1607. Died 1693. Introduced the pendulum to Britain 1658. Most important clockmaker of all.

Fromanteel, Ahasuerus and John. Sons of above. Transferred to Amsterdam c.1680.

Gould, Christopher. Died 1718. Famous for longcase, bracket clocks and watches.

Knibb, John and Joseph. Sons of Samuel Knibb. A famous name in lantern clocks and longcase clocks.

Loomes, Thomas. London clockmaker from 1649–65. Mainly known for lantern clocks.

Quare, Daniel. Born 1649. Died 1724. Famous clockmaker, known for longcase, bracket clocks and watches.

Tompion, Thomas. Born 1639. Died 1713. Best known if not most famous English clockmaker, known for lantern and longcase clocks, but principally made watches.

Windmills, Joseph. Worked in London from 1671–c.1723, known for lantern and longcase clocks.

Provincial

Bellman, William. Lancashire. Working 1790–c.1812.

Benson, Whitehaven. Working from c.1750–98.

Clifton, John. Liverpool. Working from 1777–94.

Crofts, Thomas. Leeds. Working 1752–56.

Finney, John, Joseph I and Joseph II. Liverpool. c.1761–90

Halifax, George. Halifax. 1725–1811.

Halifax, John, Joseph and Thomas. Barnsley. 1695–1789.

Lister, Thomas. Halifax. 1745–1814.

Lomax, James. Blackburn. 1749–1814.

Moore, Thomas. Ipswich. c.1740–c.1756.

Nicholson, William. Whitehaven. c. 1735–65.

Nickols, Isaac. Wells. ? London c.1700–40.

Rollison, Dollif. Father and son. Halton, Leeds. c.1720–c.1790.

Rowntree, Ralph. York. 1673–? (married 1696).

Rowntree, Robert. York. Working 1822–34.

Standring, Bolton. 1712–82.

Williamson, John. Leeds c.1683–1748.

Wilson, John. Peterborough. 1757–95.

Late 17th-century brass
lantern clock by Thomas
Dyde, London. Circular dial
with engraved face, chapter
ring with subsidiary seconds
ring with central alarm set,
posted frame with urn finials,
pierced and engraved dolphin
cresting pieces. 13⅜ in/34 cm
high. £2000–3000.

Late 17th-century brass
lantern clock with circular dial
and face engraved with tulips
and leaves, posted frame with
urn finials, outside
countwheel with pendulum
swinging between two trains
14½ in/37 cm high.
£2500–3500.

A 17th-century wing lantern
clock with single steel hand
and engraved face, chapter
ring with pierced and
engraved dolphin cresting
pieces, posted frame with urn
finials, countwheel strike.
16 in/41 cm high.
£3000–3500.

Small-sized brass lantern
clock *c.*1720 by John Parkes
& William King, London,
made for the Turkish market
with decorative foliate
spandrels, Islamic numerals,
posted frame with urn finials.
9 in/23 cm high.
£800–1200.

A 17th-century lantern clock by Thomas Wheeler c.1700 with narrow chapter ring, single hand, engraved face, dolphin cresting pieces, posted frame with urn finials. 15¾in/40cm high. £1500–2000.

An 18th-century brass lantern clock, the posted frame surmounted by a bell cage (bell lacking), the dial with brass chapter signed *Geo. Tyler, London*, now fitted with a 19th-century twin fusée movement with anchor escapement. 9in/23cm high. £500–600.

Early 18th-century brass lantern clock by Step Harris, Tonbridge. Wide chapter ring of 'sheep's head' provincial proportions, chapter outside countwheel strike. 15in/38cm high. £1200–1500.

A 19th-century lantern alarum clock with 30-hour movement by William Flint, Ashford. Posted frame, arched silvered dial with engraved decorative spandrels, central alarum dial, single hand and bell strike. 8¼in/21cm high. £900–1200.

Wall-mounted

Late 17th-century walnut wall clock with dolphin cresting piece in the arch, square dial, sliding hood, narrow chapter ring and cherubs' head spandrels, 30-hour movement with a quarter chime on 8 bells. *c.*1669–1718. Anchor escapement. 25⅛in/64cm high. £4000–6000.

'Act of Parliament' timepiece by J. Ireland, London. White-painted wooden dial, pendulum enclosed by black lacquer and chinoiserie case, roman and arabic numerals, late 18th-century, with 18in/46cm diameter dial. £4000–6000.

103

Above An 18th-century German wooden wall clock, the shaped painted dial with giltwood hands and centre alarm set, and with front mounted bob pendulum, the movement with wooden wheels and lantern pinions, and with pin wheel verge escapement. 1 ft 2¾ in/ 45 cm high. £1500–2500.

Early 19th-century ebonised wall bracket clock by Thwaites & Reed with applied brass mouldings, decorative pierced spandrels and arch decoration with fusee movement, mounted on wall bracket, with carrying-handle, *c*.1820. Anchor escapement. 16⅛ in/ 41 cm high, 2 ft 2 in/ 66 cm overall. £1000–1500.

Georgian mahogany and inlaid longcase clock, the pagoda topped hood with eagle and ball finials, flanked by reeded corinthian columns, the 13 in/33 cm painted dial with subsidiaries for seconds and for date, signed *Bancroft, Scarbro'* and with moonphase in the arch, the twin train movement with anchor escapement.
7 ft 11½ in/2.42 m.
£1000–1500.

An 18th-century red lacquer and chinoiserie longcase clock by George Washbourne, Gloucester with simplified 'pagoda-topped' hood with brass finials. 12 in/30 cm arched brass dial, subsidiary seconds and date rings, twin train 8-day five pillar movement with anchor escapement and inside countwheel strike.
7 ft 9½ in/2.38 m high.
£2500–3000.

105

George II cream and apple-green lacquer longcase clock by Isaac Nickals, Wells, Norfolk *c.*1740 with arch topped hood with whale's tail cresting. 19 in/48 cm arched brass dial, silvered chapter ring with subsidiary seconds ring, calendar aperture and centre sweep seconds hand. £15 000–20 000.

Detail of dial opposite. Moon phase and high water indicator in the lunette with strike/silent lever in the arch. Four subsidiary dials indicating days of the week, month, repeat/not repeat, and strike quarters/not strike quarters.

Right The three train 8-day five pillar movement with anchor escapement and quarters striking on three bells.

Early George III green lacquered longcase clock by Benjamin Smith, Canterbury with moulded broken-arched pediment with decorative finials, the case decorated overall in red and gold lattice. 16 in/41 cm arched brass dial with subsidiary seconds ring, calendar aperture and strike/silent dial. Five pillar movement with rack strike and anchor escapement. *c.*1770.
7 ft 4½ in/2.25 m high.
£3000–4000.

Georgian mahogany longcase clock by George Taylor, Sherborne with arched hood and horned pediment. 12 in/30 cm white-painted dial with subsidiary seconds ring, calendar aperture, moon phase indicator, twin train 8-day movement with anchor escapement. 7 ft 8 in/2.35 m high. £2000–2500.

Georgian mahogany longcase clock by Thomas Harrison, Liverpool, with moulded horned pediment. 18 in/46 cm arched brass dial with silvered chapter ring and subsidiary seconds ring, engraved face, moon phase indicator in the arch. Twin train 8-day movement with anchor escapement. 7 ft 8 in/2.35 m high. £2000–3000.

George III mahogany longcase clock by Samuel Collier, Eccles, *c.*1770 with elaborate hood with decorative finials and gilded horned pediment. White enamel dial with face decorated with pastoral scene, subsidiary seconds ring and calendar aperture, with moon phase indicator in the arch. Twin train 8-day movement with anchor escapement. 7 ft 10 in / 2.40 m high. £2000–3000.

George III mahogany longcase clock by John May, Southampton with arch topped hood and decorative finials. 12 in / 30 cm arched brass dial, silvered chapter ring and face, subsidiary seconds ring, calendar aperture and strike/silent dial. Twin train 8-day movement with anchor escapement. *c.*1773. 8 ft / 2.44 m high. £3000–3500.

Georgian mahogany longcase clock by Thomas Finney, Liverpool, with horned pediment and decorative finials. 12 in/30 cm arched brass dial, silvered chapter ring, sweep centre seconds hand and calendar hand, strike/silent lever in the centre and tune indicator changing each day. Three train movement with anchor escapement and 12 bells playing music, and moon phase indicator in arch. 7 ft 7 in/2.32 m high. £4000–6000.

George III mahogany longcase clock by William Newton, Lawson-le-Willows with modified 'pagoda-topped' hood with arched dial and rococo spandrels. 18 in/46 cm diameter brass dial with silvered chapter ring, three winding squares, subsidiary seconds ring and lunette with moon phases. Musical three train movement striking on eight graduated bells. 9 ft 10 in/c.3.0 m high. £3500–4500.

Left William and Mary marquetry longcase clock by Edward Burgis, London, with square-topped hood with simple moulding and glazed bull's eye in waist panel door. 10½ in / 27 cm square brass dial and cherub spandrels with silvered chapter ring, subsidiary seconds ring, calendar aperture and strike/silent dial. Twin train month going movement with six pillars and outside countwheel strike. *c.*1690. 6 ft 9⅞ in / 2.08 m high. £8000–10 000.

Centre William and Mary marquetry longcase clock by Francis Clement, London with single steel hand and alarum with glazed bull's eye in waist panel door. 10 in / 25 cm square brass dial with calendar ring in the centre. Twin train 8-day movement with six pillars, anchor escapement and outside countwheel strike. *c.* 1677–99. £6000–8000.

Right Early 18th-century walnut veneered and seaweed marquetry longcase clock by Thomas Taylor, Holborn, with square-topped hood with simple moulding and twist-turned columns, with glazed bull's eye in waist panel door. 10½ in / 27 cm square brass dial with cherub's head spandrels, silvered chapter ring, subsidiary seconds ring and calendar aperture. Twin train 8-day five pillar movement with anchor escapement and outside countwheel strike. 6 ft 9 in / 2.05 m high. £5000–7000.

London longcase

Left Early 18th-century red lacquer longcase clock with moulded ogee cushion pediment and glazed bull's eye in waist panel door. 16 in / 41 cm square brass dial with subsidiary seconds ring, calendar aperture, alarum train and harboured winding holes. Twin train movement with turned ring pillars and anchor escapement. 6 ft 9 in/2.05 m high. £4000–6000.

Centre Early 18th-century walnut veneered and marquetry longcase clock with carved pediment and applied cresting piece and twist-turned columns, glazed bull's eye in waist panel door. 10¾ in / 27.5 cm square brass dial with silvered chapter ring, subsidiary seconds ring and calendar aperture, with matted finish to centre of brass face. Twin train 8-day movement with five pillars, anchor escapement and inside countwheel strike. 7 ft 4 in/2.24 m high. £8000–12 000.

Right An 18th-century walnut veneered and seaweed marquetry longcase by William Sellers, Long Acre with square-topped hood and glazed bull's eye in waist panel door. 12 in / 30 cm square brass dial, crown and putti spandrels, silvered chapter ring, subsidiary seconds ring, calendar aperture. Twin train five pillar movement, month-going with bolt and shutter maintaining power, anchor escapement and outside countwheel strike. 7 ft 1 in/2.16 m high. £6000–8000.

An 18th-century walnut veneered longcase clock by Obadiah Gardner, London with square-topped hood. 16 in / 41 cm arched brass dial with silvered chapter ring, subsidiary seconds ring, calendar aperture and rise and fall regulation lever within arch. Twin train 8-day movement with anchor escapement. *c.*1712–27. 6 ft 11 in / 2.11 m high. £2800–3500.

Queen Anne burr elm longcase clock with arch-topped hood and glazed bull's eye in waist panel door. 18 in / 46 cm arched brass dial with mask and foliate spandrels, silvered chapter ring, subsidiary seconds ring, and calendar aperture. 8-day movement with anchor escapement. 7 ft 2½ in / 2.2 m high. £2000–3000.

Georgian mahogany longcase clock with ogee pediment and arch-topped hood. 12 in/30 cm arched brass dial with strike/silent indicator in arch. Silvered chapter ring and subsidiary seconds ring and calendar aperture. Twin train 8-day movement with anchor escapement. £3000–4000.

An 18th-century mahogany longcase clock, the earlier 12 in/30 cm arched brass dial with engraved wheatsheaf border, with silvered chapter ring, signed *Samuel Guy, London*, with subsidiary seconds, date aperture and ringed winding holes, the five pillared movement with inside countwheel strike. 7 ft 4 in/2.24 m high. £1000–1500.

115

Georgian mahogany longcase clock by Samuel Toulmin, London with ogee pediment and decorative finials. Arched Bilston enamel dial signed Samuel Toulmin, Strand, London. Subsidiary seconds ring and strike/silent lever in arch. Twin train 8-day movement with anchor escapement. 8 ft 6 in/2.6 m high. £3000–4000.

George III mahogany longcase clock by James McCabe, Royal Exchange, London c.1781 with arch-topped case and circular 11 in/28 cm white-painted dial with numeral sweep. An 8-day movement with anchor escapement and single strike bell. 6½ ft/2 m high. £3000–4000.

Late Victorian rosewood and ivory inlaid longcase clock with arch-topped hood and decorative pediment. 19 in / 48 cm repoussé brass dial with lacquered brass indicators and applied silver numerals. Month-going three train movement with musical chime striking on eight cylindrical gongs. £2000–3000.

Detail of dial.

117

Early 18th-century ebonised bracket clock, the case with pierced basket top surmounted by a carrying handle and decorated with four turned finials, the arched brass dial with silvered chapter ring, mock pendulum and date apertures and with subsidiaries above for strike/silent and for rise and fall regulation, signed on a cartouche, *James Snelling, London*, the six pillared movement with pull quarter repeating on six bells, verge escapement and fully engraved backplate. 1 ft 6 in/ 46 cm high £3000–4000.

Late 17th-century basket-topped bracket clock by Langley Bradley, London, with square brass dial and cherub spandrels, with the basket-top chased with scrolls and cherubs. Silvered chapter ring, calendar aperture, fusee movement with pull quarter repeat. 13¾ in/35 cm high. £3000–4000.

Early 18th-century bracket timepiece with gilt metal mounts to the cushion-topped case and S-scroll carrying handle, with oblong side glasses. 6 in/15 cm square brass dial with cherub spandrels, silvered chapter ring and pendulum aperture, pull quarter repeat and verge escapement. 15¾ in/40 cm high. £2000–3000.

George III ebonised bracket clock by Jasper Taylor, Holborn, with moulded cushion-topped case and brass carrying handle, chased spandrels, calendar and pendulum apertures and strike/silent indicator in arch. Fusee movement with verge escapement and pull quarter repeat with chimes on six bells. 17¾ in / 45 cm high. £1800–2500.

George III lacquer bracket clock by Jos. Herring, London *c*.1767 with cushion-topped case and brass carrying handle. Chased spandrels, calendar aperture and pendulum aperture with fusee movement and verge escapement. 17¾ in / 45 cm high. £3000–5000.

Ebonised bracket clock by Edward East, London *c*.1735 with cushion-topped case with carrying handle and flame and urn finials. Arched brass dial with chased spandrels, calendar aperture and pendulum aperture with strike/silent indicator in arch. Fusee movement with verge escapement and added quarter strike on six bells. 17¾ in / 45 cm high. £2000–3000.

Bracket

Ebony veneered bracket clock by Francis Gregg, Covent Garden with moulded bell-topped case and gilt brass carrying handle. 7 in / 18 cm arched brass dial with silvered chapter ring, calendar aperture and subsidiary dials for pendulum adjustment and strike no quarters/no hours/strike all. Three train movement with latched plates and dial, chiming quarters on six bells. (Later anchor escapement). 18⅞ in / 48 cm high. £3000–4000.

Late Georgian scarlet lacquer bracket clock by Frederick Miller, Chelsea, with pagoda-topped case and fretted brass side pieces. 7 in / 18 cm silvered dial with engraved decoration and strike/silent indicator in arch. Twin train movement with anchor escapement. 20 in / 51 cm high. £4500–5500.

Georgian style mahogany bracket clock, the arched case, surmounted by a carrying handle, decorated with two raised panels, the circular enamel dial with subsidiary strike/silent above, the twin fusée movement with verge escapement and engraved backplate. 1 ft 1 in / 33 cm high. £1200–1800.

Bracket

Regency musical bracket clock in ebony and ormulu with urn finials and central pineapple finial by Spencer & Perkins, London. White enamel dial and subsidiary dials for calendar and tune selection, three train fusee movement with verge escapement striking tunes on ten bells, with pull repeat. 2 ft 3⅛ in / 69 cm high. £3000–4000.

Regency mahogany bracket clock with pagoda-top, by James McCabe, London with cut brass inlaid decoration, silvered face with strike/silent indicator and pendulum adjustment dial. Three train fusee movement with anchor escapement, chiming quarters on eight bells. 2 ft 7 in / 79 cm high. £3500–4500.

George III provincial mahogany bracket clock by John Curle, Kelso with moulded caddy-topped case, arched brass dial with painted lunette with moon phase indicator. Three train fusee movement with anchor escapement. £1100–1800.

George III mahogany bracket clock by Dwerrihouse & Carter, London with arch-topped case and carrying handle *c.*1808–15. Strike/silent subsidiary dial and pendulum adjustment dial in arch, with fusee movement and anchor escapement with pull repeat. 15⅜ in/39 cm high. £2000–2500.

Small-sized ebonised bracket clock by Johnson, London with arch-topped case and carrying handle, chased spandrels, silvered chapter ring and subsidiary dials for chime/silent and slow/fast in arch. Three train fusee movement with anchor escapement chiming quarters on eight bells. 14⅜ in/36.5 cm high. £2000–3000.

Regency mahogany bracket clock by John Sheldrake, Norwich with lion's mask side handles and moulded gadroon-topped case with carrying handle. Fusee movement and anchor escapement. 17¾ in/45 cm high. £800–1200.

Regency mahogany timepiece with ebony stringing and side carrying handles with lancet-shaped case and circular white enamel dial. Fusee movement and anchor escapement.
13 in / 33 cm high.
£500–700.

Small-sized Regency mahogany bracket clock by James McCabe, Royal Exchange *c.* 1781 with architectural pediment, arched side glass and engine-turned dial. Fusee movement and later lever escapement. 9¼ in / 23.5 cm high. £500–700.

A 19th-century walnut bracket clock by French, Royal Exchange, with elaborately-carved case with Prince of Wales' Feathers, ears of corn and leaves. Engraved silvered dial, three train fusee movement and quarter strike on eight bells. £800–1200.

123

A 19th-century rosewood clock by Viner, London with circular white enamel dial, fusee movement, anchor escapement and pull repeat. 13 in/33 cm high. £600–800.

Ebonised miniature bracket clock by Dwerrihouse & Carter, London with arched silvered face and carrying handle to case. Fretted side panels, strike/silent dial below the dial, fusee movement and anchor escapement c.1780–1815. 7⅞ in/20 cm high. £1000–1500.

A 19th-century mahogany bracket clock, the arched case flanked by ring handles with brass inlaid decoration on ball feet, the painted dial with strike silent above, the twin fusée movement with anchor escapement. 1 ft 5 in/43 cm. £400–600.

Left Regency mahogany regulator timepiece by James McCabe, Royal Exchange, London. 12 in/30 cm circular dial and subsidiary dials for hours and seconds. Centre sweep minute hand, six pillar movement with maintaining power and dead-beat escapement. Pendulum suspended from 'A' bracket mounted on seat board with screw adjustment. *c*.1781. 6 ft 8¼ in/2.04 m high. £5000–7000.

Centre A 19th-century regulator timepiece by Tydeman, Stowmarket with 12 in/30 cm silvered dial, sweep centre minute hand and subsidiary dials for hours and seconds. 8-day movement with dead-beat escapement and maintaining power, glazed mercurial pendulum with beat pendulum adjustment and mirrored backboard. 6 ft 1½ in/1.87 m high. £2500–4000.

Right Victorian ebonised regulator timepiece with dead-beat escapement and maintaining power. Silvered skeleton chapter ring and subsidiary dials for seconds and hours, with glazed mercurial pendulum. 6 ft 4 in/1.93 m high. £3000–4000.

Carriage timepiece in heavy cast brass case by Barwise, London with central carrying handle with lion's mask sockets and anthemion and acanthus-leaf decoration *c.*1790. Engine-turned silver dial with fusée movement and lever escapement. 5⅞in/15 cm high. £2000–3000.

Fine mid-19th-century English engraved gilt-brass carriage clock by James McCabe, London with Corinthian column supports. Twin train chain fusée movement, typical lever escapement, striking and repeating hours on gong. Silvered dial and blue steel hands. *c.* 1781. £6000–8000.

English brass carriage clock, the twin fusée movement with lever platform escapement, striking on a gong with maintaining power and push repeat, the later case with engraved silvered dial within an engraved mask, with bevelled glass top and sides. 8½in/21.5 cm high. £1500–2000.

Decorative carriage timepiece by Finnegans, London, in silver and tortoiseshell case inlaid with floral decoration with carrying handle on small ball feet. 4½in/11.5 cm high. £400–600.

French carriage clock in 'corniche' case with lever movement and five-minute repeat. 5¼ in / 13.5 cm high. £400–600.

French carriage clock with elaborately decorated surround to dial, with five minute repeat and push repeat and lever movement. 5⅞ in / 15 cm high. £300–500.

Miniature brass carriage clock or 'mignonette' with white enamel dial and subsidiary date dial, lever movement and push repeat. 2⅞ in / 7.2 cm high. £400–500.

Carved ebonised carriage clock by Charles Frodsham, London with silvered dial within an engraved foliate brass surround with fusee movement and lever escapement. £1800–2500.

Mahogany mantel clock of waisted balloon shape by Metcalf, London c.1781–1825. White enamel dial with subsidiary seconds ring, fusee movement and anchor escapement. 18¾ in / 47.5 cm high. £2000–3000.

Early Regency balloon clock by Johnson, Grey's Inn Passage, London in mahogany with moulded ogee pediment and pineapple finial and dummy side carrying handles. Fusee movement and anchor escapement. 17¾ in / 45 cm high. £1500–2000.

Late 18th-century early balloon-shaped timepiece by Weeks, Coventry Street, c.1790 with brass drum case and white enamel dial on painted decorative base with pierced brass skirt and curving scroll feet. 15⅜ in / 39 cm high. £1000–1500.

A 19th-century brass skeleton timepiece with single train movement, narrow silvered chapter ring, platform and lever escapement. 12½ in/32 cm high. £550–750.

Right A 19th-century brass skeleton timepiece, the scroll plates with silvered chapter ring, the fusée movement with six spoked wheels, and anchor escapement, on four turned supports, on an oval white marble base. 17¾ in/45 cm high. £500–700.

Fine brass skeleton timepiece of Gothic design by Vaughan, Bristol, on marble plinth. Fusee movement and anchor escapement. 15 in/38 cm high. £800–1200.

A 19th-century rosewood four-glass mantel clock by Dent, London, with silvered face and engraved spandrels. Fusee movement with anchor escapement, strike/silent bar and pull repeat. 11⅜ in/29 cm high £1500–2000.

A 19th-century French tortoiseshell and inlaid mantel clock, the rectangular surmounted by a carrying handle, the circular movement now with lever escapement striking on a bell with outside countwheel strike, signed *Paul Garnier, H^{er} Du Roi Paris*, and numbered 1076, with gilt dial. 9 in/23 cm high. £350–450.

Victorian Boulle mantel clock veneered in tortoiseshell and cut brass with enamel numerals to the decorative brass face, with heavy ormolu mounts in rococo style. 18½ in/47 cm high. £700–1000.

Louis XVI mantel clock with
allegorical figures flanking a
plain enamel dial
surmounted by clouds and
doves. 14⅛ in / 36 cm high.
£800–1200.

A 19th-century rosewood
mantel clock, the rectangular
case glazed to the top and
sides with brass inlaid canted
angles above an ogee
moulding on bun feet, the
square silvered dial with
engraved spandrels, signed
Jⁿᵒ Jones, London, the twin
fusée movement with anchor
escapement. 1 ft 1¾ in / 35 cm
high. £600–800.

Ormolu mantel timepiece in
the shape of a classical urn by
Grant, Fleet Street with
white enamel dial, fusee
movement and anchor
escapement. 10¼ in / 26 cm
high. £1800–2500.

131

Art Deco

A German brass mantel clock, the circular copper face with black enamelled numerals and hands mounted in a brass case of flattened circular form on brass supports with bevelled glass panels on a rectangular base. 15½ in/ 39 cm high. £200–250.

A stylish 'Egyptianesque' figural timepiece, the circular face with roman numerals flanked by outspread wings in gilt and blue patination, mounted on a massive block of green onyx before which an Egyptianesque girl in gilt, blue and brown patinated/bronze adopts a stylish pose, the whole raised on a brown variegated rectangular marble base. 20 in/51 cm high. £1800–2300.

A Liberty & Co. 'English Pewter' timepiece, designed by Archibald Knox, the upright rectangular case having circular face with copper-coloured numerals with red-enamelled 'berry' forms against shaded blue and green enamelling, flanked by stylised entrelacs, leaves and berries. 8 in/20.5 cm high. £1200–1600.

Silver

Techniques and tools

The techniques and tools of the silversmith have changed remarkably little down the centuries, and craftsmen who make silver by hand today use much the same methods as silversmiths did generations ago. Until the end of the 17th century, English silver was largely made from sheet metal, laboriously beaten out from ingots and then hammered and shaped. The hollow part of a bowl, jug, dish or pot was made in one piece from sheet silver which was hammered out in a 'sinking block' until the shape of a shallow bowl was achieved, and then over a 'raising stake', until the shallow bowl was transformed into the body of a vessel.

An alternative method used from the late 17th century for making hollow ware was to shape a piece of sheet metal into a cone or cylinder, seam it together with solder and then hammer it into shape. This method was used for straight-sided tankards, mugs and coffee pots and the seam can sometimes be detected as a faint hairline, usually following the line of the handle. Vessels made in this way were finished with a sprung wire round the rim. All the additional parts – foot rim, handle, girdle, spout or decoration – were 'applied' or soldered on to the body.

Any parts not soldered but detachable had to be assayed and marked. Thus the lids of covered tankards and cups have a separate set of marks, as do lids of coffee pots and teapots. Some heavy-cast decorative borders of salvers and tazza ware are not soldered but simply joined, and heavy cast handles of soup tureens are usually bolted to the lids. Any finials which unscrew and any stands which are detachable or made as a separate entity, and sometimes even cast feet must all have the 'sterling' mark of the lion passant at least, if not a complete set of marks. Obviously, all the marks on the various parts of a single piece must be of the same period if it is genuine and authentic.

English silver plate

Gold and silver have been collectively known as 'plate' since Elizabethan days. The name is derived from the Spanish 'plata' which actually means silver. In its pure form, silver, like gold, is too soft to endure, and has always been alloyed with small quantities of harder metal, usually copper with which it has an affinity. In England, the standard proportion of pure silver which constitutes 'sterling' silver is 92.5 per cent pure silver and was first laid down in 1300 by King Edward I. Apart from a brief period from 1697–1720 this standard has remained unchanged to this day. Gold and silver are weighed in Troy weight, slightly different from avoirdupois or metric, and includes the archaic 'dwt' or pennyweight. One Troy ounce is equal to 20 dwt and represents 0.9115 of one ounce avoirdupois.

These weights and measures are important to the potential buyer of antique silver – or indeed any sterling silver – because when the weight of an object is quoted it represents the silver alloy and not the pure silver alone, which will be 7.5 per cent less than the total weight. This is also a point to remember when comparing the price of antique silver with the bullion price quoted on financial pages which is of course for pure silver.

From the earliest times until towards the end of the 19th century, silver was extracted from its ore by a process known as 'leaching' which removed all impurities except for any gold there might be. After 1884 silver was extracted by an electrolytic process and contains no trace of any other elements at all. Almost all antique silver contains minute traces of gold, and it may be this factor which gives old silver a bloom and depth of shine which is not found in silver extracted by modern methods.

Styles and periods

Early English silver (up to c. 1700)

The massive style of Continental silver seems to have had little influence on English silversmiths, at least until the end of the 17th century. Designs were simple and decoration showed the Dutch influence which came to England with the return of Charles II from The Hague in 1660, and then with William of Orange in 1688. Decorative motifs were mostly of flowers and leaves, embossed, chased or punched into the sheet metal, and little cast decoration was applied or added. Cut-card work was used to great effect by English silversmiths from the latter years of the 17th and early 18th centuries. A sheet of silver was cut or pierced in a decorative design and then soldered round the body or rim of a vessel, sometimes as a decorative border, often in the shape of a calyx or as leaves cupping the base.

From the 1680s onwards there was a fashion for 'chinoiserie' and oriental designs were often engraved on grander silverware. Armorials and cartouches were also engraved on silver belonging to the nobility and the gentry. In 1685, threats of religious persecution brought many Huguenot silversmiths to England who brought with them techniques which had not been used by English silversmiths before, as well as introducing the grander, heavier shapes and designs of Continental silverware.

Queen Anne (c.1700–30)

The great period of Queen Anne silver was the result of a marriage between the simple lines of English silver and the casting and working techniques brought over by the Huguenots. At this period too, the social fabric of England was changing and there was a great demand for silver of all kinds. The custom of tea and coffee drinking, the fashion for matching tableware, the advent of forks, the need for sauces for a changing cuisine, all meant a whole magnificent array of table silver for the prosperous merchants and landed gentry. Shapes were still simple, decoration still restrained. Form was based on the cyma curve and the baluster, more curving than the tapering cylindrical shapes of the previous centuries. Candlesticks were still cast in solid silver, and all pieces were of heavier gauge than earlier English silver.

Rococo (c.1730-50)

As the century advanced, the shape of silver became more sinuous. Straight spouts vanished in favour of high curved ones, often with heads of animals, handles were scrolled, plain foot rims were replaced with small scrolling feet. With the curves came more ornament: gadrooning and shells, scrolls and foliage, paw feet and lion's masks. Around 1730 these motifs erupted into full-blown rococo, in a fashion which emanated from France, principally from the designs of court silversmith Juste Aurèle Meissonier. Cartouches became assymetrical, there was a return to 'chinoiserie', swirling bases to candlesticks and flambeau finials added to the feeling of movement, so different from the plain and simple lines of Queen Anne silver.

Classical (c.1750-1800)

With the return of classicism under the all-pervading influence of the Adam brothers, English silver underwent a radical change. The baluster shape on which so much silver design had been based was swept away in favour of classical urns, vases and columns, decorated with swags and festoons, rams' heads, classical medallions, anthemion, formalised scrolls and leaves. There were helmet-shaped cream jugs and sugar bowls with pedestal feet and swing handles, vase-shaped tea caddies and teapots, all richly engraved with classical themes. Towards the end of the century 'bright cut' engraving produced a more brilliant, almost three-dimensional effect and became the principal method of surface decoration until the end of the century and beyond. Machines for stamping and rolling came into use, resulting in thinner gauge silver for the wider market, and candlesticks were made from stamped sheet metal, wholly or partly, and filled with pitch, known as 'loaded' candlesticks.

Regency (c.1800-30)

As with Sheraton furniture, by the end of the 18th century much of the silver made for the general market had been prettified rather than simplified into light and airy shapes and designs, decorated with garlands rather than swags. This tendency was soon to be reversed in favour of the massive, the grand and the sculptural. It was an age which was unsurpassed for craftsmanship and quality, during which many of the massive centrepieces and banqueting services were made which can be seen on display in stately homes today. This was the period of John Flaxman and the great 'Shield of Achilles' manufactured by Rundell, Bridge & Rundell, measuring 36½ in / 92.71 cm in diameter, and weighing 669 oz 10 dwt and of basins and ewers, sideboard dishes, tureens, entrée dishes and dessert stands embellished with freestanding decoration, cast and applied in spectacular style. The severity of earlier classical shapes gave way to more curving lines, with campana-shaped wine coolers and cisterns and melon-shaped teapots and tea services. Table silver too became much heavier, and to the old relatively plain patterns of Old English,

Silver

Hanoverian and traditional rat-tailed patterns were added scrolled heavyweight King's pattern, Queen's pattern and Coburg, amongst others.

Victorian (c.1830–1900)

With so much ornament balancing on a knife-edge between the opulent and the vulgar, it was almost inevitable that decline should follow. But although a great deal of silver made during this period was overblown and ostentatious, some extremely fine 'Queen Anne' silver was made, as well as some excellent and original designs which sprang from the Arts & Crafts Movement and Art Nouveau. The period spans so many decades and covers so many changes in manufacturing techniques one should not attempt to generalise. A lot of Victorian silver which looks heavy is in fact made of thin-gauge silver, spun, stamped or embossed by machine, but individual craftsmen were still making fine quality silver with traditional methods, and amongst the proliferation of objects, there is still much to be found of fine workmanship and design.

Edwardian (c.1900–20)

There was a little innovation during this period with the exception of some Art Nouveau silver, but many of the reproductions of earlier designs were excellently made in heavy gauge silver by well-established companies such as the Goldsmiths & Silversmiths, Garrards, Mappin & Webb and Aspreys. Dangerous to those who do not know it, is the technique of 'acid-engraving', similar to that used for making plates for printing, and recognizable by its shallow, dull appearance.

Sheffield plate

Sheffield Plate is also known as 'Old Sheffield' and was first made in the 1740s. Thin layers of sterling silver are fused to sheets of copper by heating both metals and then rolling them together. Originally used for making small objects such as buttons, buckles and boxes, once the technique was perfected, almost any item made in silver could be made in Sheffield Plate. From about 1768 silver wire was made by the same process and many really remarkable openwork and wirework epergnes, baskets and sweetmeat dishes were produced which do not have their equivalent in sterling silver. By the last decade of the 18th century it was quite customary for some items of table silver, such as soup tureens, to be accompanied by a stand made of cheaper Sheffield Plate.

The marking of Sheffield Plate however is a quagmire of complications and needs special study and the advice of an expert to be properly understood. It is a subject well worth investigating, for today Sheffield Plate is considerably less expensive than sterling silver and many pieces are every bit as worthy of display.

Electroplating

This process was first patented in 1840 and employed the principal of electrical deposition of gold or silver on to a base metal. Unlike Sheffield Plate, the silver had to be pure, and differs in colour by being bluer and colder than sterling silver. Apart from the fact that this process meant that all kinds of objects could be cast and made in a variety of base metals and then coated in silver, it also made it possible for 'repairs' of a dubious nature to be covered up with a layer of silver – a possibility which fakers and forgers were not slow to realize.

Electrotyping

This is an extension of electroplating, and employs a mould or cast on which the silver is deposited. An extremely costly process, it was used for making very restricted numbers of copies of such famous pieces as John Flaxman's 'Shield of Achilles'. Its merit is that the cast remains as crisp from the first copy to the last, unlike an ordinary cast or mould whose modelling blurs with use.

Marks and hallmarks

Strictly speaking, there is only one actual 'hallmark' on a piece of silver – a leopard's head, crowned or uncrowned, ordained by statute in 1300 when the standard of purity for sterling silver was laid down. But there should be at least four marks on all but the smallest pieces of silver. Apart from the leopard's head there should be a maker's mark, added by law in 1363 and usually the initials of the silversmith, and a date letter, incorporated in 1478. This device, a brilliantly simple way of identifying the Assayer in case of dishonesty or corruption, has become a remarkable and unbroken record, enabling silver to be dated year by year through more than five centuries. The letter changes annually through a twenty year cycle, omitting 'J' and 'V' to 'Z' and each cycle has a different type letter and surround. The London Assay Office began the year in May – provincial offices do not necessarily coincide with London until 1975 when all Assay Offices in Britain agreed to a single date, changed annually on 1 January.

The fourth mark is that of the 'lion passant' and was added in 1544 as a further protection against the adulteration of silver. The various styles of this mark can also help with dating: originally the lion was 'passant guardant' a heraldic term denoting walking with its head turned to regard i.e. full face. The style and surround changed down the centuries and provide a broad indication of period. From 1822 the lion was redesigned in profile but still walking and became simply 'passant'.

In addition to these four marks, between 1784 and 1890 a sovereign's head was added to denote that duty had been paid and these too, apart from the identity of the reigning monarch, add to the verification of authenticity.

If a piece of silver was not made in London but in the provinces, the mark of the provincial assay office will also be struck, as well as the leopard's head in Chester, York, Newcastle and Exeter up to 1777 but not later, and without the leopard's head in Birmingham and Sheffield.

Britannia Standard

One further mark occurs on a limited number of pieces, between the years 1697 and 1720. During this period the standard proportions for silver were changed to increase the pure metal content to 95.8 per cent. It was marked with the

Silver

figure of Britannia instead of the sterling 'lion passant' and known as 'Britannia Standard'. During those years too, the leopard's head was also removed and a 'lion's head erased' substituted. Another heraldic term meaning a lion's head in profile, with a ragged edge to the neck. The pure silver content is higher and calculations for Britannia Standard is the total weight less 4.2 per cent base metal alloy.

Fakes and forgeries

From 1720 when duty was first imposed even reputable silversmiths transposed marks from a small piece on which tax had really been paid to a larger one to avoid paying duty. These pieces are known as 'duty dodgers' and although at one time illegal, are now bought and collected as oddities in themselves, providing they have been reassayed and found up to sterling standard. Modern fakers and forgers who transpose marks cannot match old silver with new and often resort to electroplating the completed piece with the marks soldered in place in order to conceal the deception. Since electroplating uses pure silver, a simple test will detect this practice: nitric acid slightly diluted with distilled water will turn the surface of sterling silver blue (make the test where it cannot be seen). With pure silver there is no change in colour, therefore it has been electroplated.

Casting up a pair from a genuine single to increase the value can be detected by the fact that every detail including hallmarks are identically placed. In genuine pairs hallmarks never match up in alignment and position.

The common practice of 'improving' silver, thereby reducing its value, was most prevalent in the Victorian era. Plain early silver was embossed and chased with decorative motifs to increase its attraction, and flat-chasing was added to the surface of plain salvers and trays. The removal and addition of armorials is another practice frequently encountered. Probably for reasons of snobbery, old family crests were removed and evidence of 'second hand' silver was thus removed, and a layer of silver with it, thus reducing its value. Newly acquired armorials brashly engraved on pieces of genuine old family silver also reduces the value of a piece.

Provincial, Scottish and Irish Assay Office marks

Birmingham	An anchor.
Chester	A shield with three half-lions and wheatsheaves until 1779: after that three wheatsheaves and a sword.
Dublin	A harp.
Edinburgh	A triple-towered castle.
Exeter	Three towers.
Glasgow	A tree and a salmon.
Newcastle-upon-Tyne	Three towers, two above and one below.
Norwich	A castle above a lion or a crowned Tudor rose, both rare.
Sheffield	A crown, sometimes repeated in the date letter.
York	A cross incorporating five lions.

Silver

The various marks would make it seem a simple matter to date and identify a piece of silver, but reading these marks requires considerable skill and knowledge. There is a difference in each cycle of the alphabet, both in the shape of the letter and the surround, often difficult to differentiate. The 'lion passant guardant' changes in design, and so does the leopard's head and the sovereign's head. All the marks must accord, not with wishful thinking, but accurately with the date assumed. Only time and a great deal of experience will provide the ability to read silver marks accurately.

Top Victorian oblong box, the cover chased in low relief with a pastural scene, cows grazing and rabbits in the foreground, musicians and bulrushes in the foreground, by F. B. Thomas, 1879. 7¼ × 5¼ in/18.4 × 13.3 cm. £500–700.
Above George III silver gilt snuff box with classical scene of the philosopher Diogenes. By Joseph Ash, 1813. 3 in/7.5 cm. £500–600.

Leading silversmiths

Angell, Joseph 1811–24 and son John Angell 1824–c.1850. Well-known maker of tea and coffee sets.

Barnard, Emes & Barnard 1808–29. Messrs. Barnard from 1829. High quality ware, and many important table centrepieces and cups.

Bateman, Hester 1761–90. Domestic silver of high quality, with the workshop continuing with Peter and Jonathon, Ann, William and William II.

Boulton, Matthew Birmingham metalworker and silversmith, in association with John Fothergill, and with many leading designers, making high quality silverware, Sheffield plate and ormolu from 1784, the business continued until 1819.

Cafe, John Specialist candlestick maker from 1740–57, followed by his brother William until c.1775.

Chawner, Henry 1786–1810. High quality silverware, especially teapots and tea ware, in partnership with John Emes 1796–1810.

Coker, Ebenezer 1738–c.1780. Candlestick maker, salvers and chambersticks.

de Lamerie, Paul 1713–51. The most famous London silversmith, particularly associated with rococo style, as well as more simple items.

Elkington & Co. Birmingham. Famous makers in 19th century, probably best known for electrotyping and electroplating.

Emes, John. In partnership with Barnard, see above.

Farrell, Edward 1813–35. Copyist of early styles and maker of typically-associated florid Victorian wares.

Fogelberg, Andrew c.1770–c.1800. Master of Paul Storr.

Fox, Charles son of Charles Fox I working c.1822–c.1840. Produced many items associated with the Dutch style, workshop continued with George Fox until c.1860.

Garrard, Robert 1792–1818. Good quality silverware, the business continuing with his son Robert II from 1818–53.

Gould, James 1722–47. Candlestick maker, as well as his son William 1732–56.

Hennell, Robert 1763–1811. One of a large dynasty of silvermakers, including his father David, and sons David Hennell II and Samuel, and grandson Robert, working until 1868.

Hunt & Roskell. A 19th-century workshop producing work of famous designers such as Paul Storr, Flaxman.

Platel, Pierre 1697–1719. Huguenot silversmith famous for work of highest quality, master of Paul de Lamerie who was his apprentice.

Scofield 1776–96. One of the finest silversmiths of his period, making fine quality designs of great craftsmanship.

Smith, Benjamin 1802–18. Designed and worked almost exclusively for Rundell, Bridge and Rundell, making work of extremely high quality.

Storr, Paul 1792–1838. Maker and designer of sumptuous high quality silver, for Rundell, Bridge and Rundell as well as more delicate items.

Willaume, David 1697–1728. Huguenot silversmith working in England, the business continuing with his son David Willaume II from 1728–c.1746.

Wood, Samuel 1733–c.1773. Specialist caster maker.

Commonwealth sweetmeat dish with scalloped handles and punched decoration. *c.*1654. 6⅛ in / 15.5 cm diameter. £800–1200.

Commonwealth wine taster with looped wire handles and punched pineapple decoration. *c.*1655. 4¾ in / 12 cm diameter. £700–900.

Charles II beaker with embossed and flat-chased decoration and applied foot-rim. 1683. 5½ in / 14 cm high. £1500–2500.

Charles II bleeding bowl with cast pierced handle, possibly by William Gamble 1682. 5⅜ in / 14 cm diameter. £1500–2500.

George I two-handled lemon strainer by Thomas Keddon.
1715. £800–1100.

Charles II beaker, of thistle
form, the upper part chased
with stylised frieze of seeded
flowers and leaves, a rope
border below the rim, the
latter pricked with an earlier
dated inscription: *CF to WT
Bapt Feb 27th 1646.* 3½ in/
9 cm high, punched four
times with the letters TD for
Thomas Dare, Junior, and
the T & Tun mark for
Taunton, *c.* 1660. £1000–
2000.

Charles II porringer
embossed and chased with
lion and unicorn with
flowerheads and cast
handles. 1683.
3¾ in/9.5 cm high.
£2500–4000.

William III two-handled
porringer with gadrooned
decoration by Robert
Timbrell 1703. £1200–1800.

George I casters of octagonal
baluster shape with engraved
armorials, one pierced, one
blind. 6½ in / 16 cm high.
Pair: £1500–1800.
Single: £750–1000.

Queen Anne sugar caster of
baluster form with applied
girdle, pierced decoration
and bayonet fitting by
Christopher Canner I. 1707.
8 in / 20.5 cm high.
£1200–1500.

Left George II caster of
baluster shape and rococo
design by Samuel Wood.
1758. 2½ in / 6 .25 cm.
£450–650.

A pair of late 19th-century
casters with applied girdles
and vineleaves by Elkington
& Co. 7 in/18 cm high.
£800–1000. (Heavy gauge)

143

Salts

George III oval salts with ramsheads, swags and beaded rims by Robert Hennell II. 1777. £500–800.

William IV salts with cast shell feet by Edward Farrell. 1833. 2¾ in/7 cm diameter. Pair: £250–300.

George III salts with cast paw feet and gadrooned rims by John Bridge. 1824. Pair: £550–750.

Victorian salts in the shape of shells on dolphin supports and seawave bases, after the style of Paul Storr. Pair: £2500–3000. Single: £1200–1500.

Victorian carved walnut and burr-veneered three-division Canterbury whatnot, cross-banded in thuya. 1 ft 11 in/58 cm. £1000–1500.

Pair of Sheraton period satinwood elbow chairs, the rectangular backs with vertical splats with roundel ornament, having cushion seats on ring turned tapered legs (2). £6000.

Walnut, crossbanded and featherstrung double-dome bureau bookcase in the Queen Anne taste, the upper part with a moulded cornice fitted with shelves, enclosed by a pair of arched glazed panel doors, the sloping fall enclosing a concave fitted graduated interior with drawers, pigeonholes and central cupboard enclosed by a panel door, containing four long drawers, on bracket feet. 6 ft 9 in/2.06 m high, 2 ft 10 in/87 cm wide. £4000–6000.

Above Victorian tulipwood crossbanded, ormolu and porcelain mounted writing table in the Louis XV taste, the top inset with a panel of shaped tooled leather, the frieze fitted with a drawer to one end and mounted with Sèvres style porcelain plaques. 3 ft 6 in × 2 ft/1.05 m × 61 cm. £4000.

A 19th-century Italian marble centre table on an ebonised gilt metal mounted tripod base, the marble top crossbanded in micro mosaic with Roman masks. £3000–5000.

A 19th-century satinwood decorated, tulipwood crossbanded and boxwood and ebony strung writing table of Carlton House type painted with oval panels of ladies and putti, scrolling foliage and musical trophies, the superstructure with ogee hinged compartments and a central enclosed cupboard flanked by drawers with three drawers below, on square tapered legs terminating in brass cappings and castors. 3 ft 10 in/1.17 m. £6000–8000.

One of a set of six George III carved mahogany and fruitwood dining chairs, in the Chippendale taste. Undulating toprails and pierced interlaced box splats with foliate scroll ornament with slip-in seat (one back leg replaced). £4000–6000.

A good 19th-century ormolu and marble mantel clock, the case of lyre form surmounted by a sunburst mask and decorated with swags on an oval base, the enamel chapter signed *Deniere à Paris*, with pierced gilt hands and centre date hand, the signed movement with outside countwheel. 2 ft 2½ in/67 cm high. £2000–3000.

Right An unusual 19th-century French gilt bronze and porcelain mounted carriage clock, the movement with replaced platform striking on a gong, with alarm and push repeat, and bearing the *Drocourt* trademark on the backplate, numbered 7526. The side panels decorated with scenes each depicting Classical maidens and a putti in a landscape. 9 in/23 cm high. £3000–4000.

Below, left to right A 19th-century French brass and enamel mounted carriage clock, the lever movement striking on a gong, with alarm and push repeat and bearing the *Drocourt* trademark, numbered 21096, the dial decorated with stylised birds and flora. 7½ in/19 cm high. £1200–1800.

A French 19th-century gilt brass and enamel carriage clock, the lever movement striking on a gong, with push repeat, and marked G.L., 1220. 7½ in/19 cm high. £800–1200.

A 19th-century French gilt brass and enamel mounted carriage clock, the lever movement striking on a gong with push repeat. 7½ in/19 cm high. £1200–1800.

Top left A Victorian mounted glass claret jug with cylindrical neck etched with star motifs, the bead-edged mount chased with flowers, scrolls and berries around an oval, crested cartouche, by W. & G. Sissons, Sheffield, 1863. 10¹/₁₆ in/25.5 cm high. £1000.

Top right A Victorian glass claret jug with diaperwork, the silver-gilt fluted mount with bead girdle beneath a band of Greek key decoration, the scalloped spout and domed, fluted cover with knop finial, by Robert Garrard, 1865. 11¾ in/30 cm. £800.

Bottom left & right A matched pair of Victorian decanters, the glass bodies with silver-gilt fruiting vine collars, handles (squeeze action) and covers, the latter with vine leaf and tendril finials, one bell-shaped with faceted sides and neck, the other of ovoid-shape with cut-out flutes and faceted neck by Riley & Storer, respectively 1847 and 1851. 12 in/30.5 cm and 12³/₁₆ in/31 cm high respectively. £2400.

Bottom centre A Victorian glass claret jug, etched with butterflies, flowers, leaves and ferns, the silver-gilt mount decorated with stylised leaves, domed cover with knop finial, by Horace Woodward, Birmingham, 1874. 11¼ in/28.5 cm high. £580.

George II silver-gilt cow creamer with textured body, the oval, hinged cover chased with flowers and applied with a fly, by John Schuppe, 1756, 5oz. £14300.

Mid-Victorian tea caddy by George Fox, the four sides of the oblong body finely chased against a matted background, with *chinoiserie* scenes depicting figures reading or walking in the background, the corners mounted with reeded posts surmounted by domed finials, the hinged cover with a scaled (bamboo) frieze, domed and chased with similar *chinoiserie* and surmounted by a cast bird finial. 1866. 6⁵⁄₁₆in/16cm high. £2000–3000.

George III unmarked armorial wine label modelled as a
demi-rampant horse charged with a fleur-de-lys upon a
narrow rectangular title scroll with rounded ends and a
feather-edge, incised 'Sherry', c.1795. £180–220.

Unmarked early 19th-century armorial wine label modelled as
an eagle crest with wings displayed charged with a cross and
pierced 'Sherry'. £300–400.

Rare George III Irish sphinx wine label, the title scroll incised
'Claret' and flanked by hieroglyphics, by James Le Bass,
Dublin, 1813. £400–600.

Two English models of cottages, Staffordshire and Yorkshire, early Victorian. *c.*£100 each.

Fine Bloor Derby bough pot and cover of bombé shape, the cover with a rich profusion of individually modelled flowers in bright enamel colours, the blue and gilt pot also applied with flowers within elaborate gilt scrollwork, standing on four scrolled feet, 7⅞ in/20 cm, Bloor Derby circular red mark. £2000–3000.

Rare and impressive London saltglazed Bellringers' jug, of plain globular form with a finely grooved cylindrical neck, slight pinched lip and strap handle, the glaze of even mid-brown tone, early 18th century. 13⅜ in/34 cm. £500–700.

Pair of Derby groups of sheep, one with a ram and lying-down lamb, the other with a ewe and suckling lamb, their fleece mostly white with russet patches, both groups with well modelled flowering bocage, on irregular white mound bases strewn with coloured flowers and leaves. 5⅝ in/14.5 cm. £1400–1600.

'The Dancer' by Doris Lindner, a very rare figure in Art Deco style modelled as a lady in stylish dancing pose, her head thrown back, her arms outstretched holding up the hem of her long diaphanous dress shaded in orange and gold sheen, on a plain circular base. Shape no. 3088, date code for 1936, inscribed title. 7⅞ in/20 cm. £400–500.

Above Two finely engraved Bohemian ruby glass goblets, mid-19th century. £2000–3000 each.

Below left A St. Louis large pelargonium paperweight, the five-petalled flower in rich blue enclosing a yellow and black dot stamen, the stalk with two lanceolate leaves, set above a swirling latticinio ground. £1000–1200.

Below right A rare St. Louis flat bouquet paperweight, the central flower with five pink petals outlined in white, surrounded by smaller flowers and buds in constrasting colours, springing from a leafy stalk, the base star-cut. £3000–4000.

Above A finely carved cameo vase, decorated in white relief with a hibiscus flower, bud and leafy branch pendant from a cushion knop carved with a border of white flowerheads, below a trumpet neck with a budding spray, probably Stevens & Williams. 10in/25.3 cm. £1800.
Below left A Baccarat garlanded butterfly paperweight, the insect with dark purple body, turquoise eyes, and well coloured wings. £1400–1600.
Below right A very rare St. Louis concentric millefiori mushroom paperweight, the central cluster of blue and green arrow-head canes encircled by rows in white and red, the base with a flange containing a red and white torsade, the foot rim with diagonally hatched staves in yellow and white, cut with top and six side printies. £1800–2200.

A Bohemian tankard, of cylindrical shape with spreading base overlaid in deep blue and engraved with a solitary stag in a woodland, the hinged pewter lid set with a glass panel inscribed J. Elliott, 1873. 10¼in/ 26cm. £300–400.

An ovoid vase attributed to Thomas Webb & Sons, with rich blue ground, decorated in white with a spray of a fully-open tiger lily with two buds and four leaf sprays, the short neck with cross-hatched border, the foot with solid white band. 5½in/14cm. £750–900.

Cream jugs and creamers

George II cream pitcher with applied cast handle, possibly by Jonathan Newton. 1736. 3 in / 7.5 cm. £500–850.

George III baluster cream jug with double-scroll handle and reverse bead punched border by Hester Bateman. 1785. £350–400.

George III cream jug with moulded pleated sides and reeded border by Peter and Anne Bateman. 1798. £150–200.

George III helmet-shaped cream jug with bright-cut decoration by Thos. Wallis II. 1802. £200–300.

Sauce and butter boats

George II sauce boat with wavy-cut border and cast shell-and-hoof feet by William Skeen. 1759. Pair: £1200–1800.

Below right George III sauce boat with gadrooned rim, cast shell feet and leaf-capped scroll handle by Smith & Sharpe. 1762. Pair: £1200–2000.

Above George III sauce boat with cast shell feet, gadrooned border and acanthus leaf handle by Fuller White. 1761. Pair: £1000–1500.

George III Irish sauce boat with shell-and-hoof feet and cast double scroll handle by Charles Townsend. Dublin 1775. Pair: £1200–1500. Single: £400–500.

Chambersticks

George III Scottish chamberstick with plain circular pan and flying scroll handle by William Drummond. Edinburgh 1767. £750–900.

A pair of George III chambersticks and extinguisher caps with gadrooned shell and foliate borders and openwork stems for snuffers by Samuel Hennell and John Terry. 1814. 4in/11.4cm high. Pair: £1200–1600.

George IV chamberstick with gadroon shell and foliate border, matching decoration to drip pan and extinguisher cap with ornate flying scroll handle, openwork stem for snuffers and rounded urn-shaped sconce by Matthew Boulton & Co. 1823. Pair: £1200–1850.

Chamberstick with deep dished pan and pierced gallery with S-scrolls with loop handle by Ramsden & Carr. 1912. £800–1200.

James II cast candlesticks with canted corners, baluster turned with reeded stems. 1688. 6¼in/15.9cm high. Pair: £10000–15000.

George II cast candlesticks with wavy-pleated bases, ribbed drip-pans and shoulder knops by John Cafe. 1749. 7¾in/19.7cm high. Pair: £2600–3200.

George III cast candlesticks of unusual design, the shaped stepped square bases with eagle-like claw motifs to the corners, the baluster stems forming the bird's legs, rope borders and girdles, the nozzles, also with 'claw' corners, engraved with a crest, possibly for *Hixon* or *Hickson*. 9⅞in/25cm high, by Ebenezer Coker, 1762. Pair: £2500–3000.

George II cast candlesticks with shell bases and engraved armorial lozenge, shell decoration to drip-pans and flared shoulder knops by Simon Jouet *c.*1755. 8½in/22cm high. Pair: £2600–3200.

George III tapersticks with square bases and acanthus leaf decoration, gadrooned shoulder knops and stamped decoration to drip-pans *c.*1770. 7¼in/18.4cm high. Pair: £2500–4500.

George III candlesticks in embossed sheet silver, baluster-shaped with heavy rococo decoration in high relief by John and Thomas Settle. Sheffield 1816. Pair: £1200–1600.

George IV candlesticks with flared shoulder knops and vestigial leaf decoration to the baluster base by S.C. Younge & Co. Sheffield 1829. Pair: £1000–1500. Loaded.

Late Victorian candlesticks based on Adam-style Corinthian column with high-stepped bases and entwined ivy up the stem, by Charles Boyton, 1891. Pair: £1000–1350. Loaded.

Plates and dishes

George IV silver-gilt fruit dish, cast in the form of a large leaf matted and realistically fashioned with veins, twig and, on the matted surface, two caterpillars, approximately 11⅜ in/29 cm diameter, probably by Jonathan Watson & Son (?), Sheffield, c. 1825. £1000–1500.

Oval meat dish with gadroon and leaf border, the most typical shape, usually made to match sets of plates, from early Georgian to Victorian. 1821. £800–1200.

Set of standard pattern dinner plates of mixed Victorian and Edwardian dates, with plain gadrooned borders and scalloped edges marked for 1839, 1849 and 1904. Half dozen: £3500–4800.

Set of soup plates of similar design with shallower gadrooning round the rims. 1849. Half dozen: £3200–4400.

Salvers and tazze

Above A pair of George I tazze on plain foot with finely engraved cartouche in the style of the period by William Gamble 1718. 10⅜ in / 26.4 cm diameter. £4000–5000. Single: £1500–1800.

Left: George II octafoil salver with gadrooned border, mounted on plain cast feet, by Louis Cuny. 1733. 9 in / 22.9 cm wide. £3250–4250.

George III Irish oval salver with reeded border and cast fluted feet by Richard Sawyer, Dublin 1799. 12½ in / 32 cm across. £1900–2250.

Victorian salver with rococo-style shell and scroll border and flat-chased base with rocaille motif on cast shell feet by William Eley II. 1839. 11¼ in / 28.5 cm diameter. £600–900.

Victorian swing handled cast pierced basket-work circular cake basket with trailing wheatsheaf rim, the base engraved with a laurel wreath, 12³/₁₆ in/31 cm diameter by Harrison Bros & Howson, Sheffield, 1857. £1500–2000.

George III swing-handled cake basket, the surface engraved with armorials, on a supporting rim, with a later inscription underneath the base, 14⁹/₁₆ in/37 cm long, by Emick Romer, 1766 (with a presentation case). £2500–3200.

A pair of Victorian wine coolers, modelled as wooden pails with two ribbons around the sides, complete with liners, by Elkington & Co. 1873. 8½ in/22 cm high. £700–1000.

William IV cake basket of circular form with pleated sides embossed and chased with flowers and foliage on pleated foot with applied cast border, and a pierced stem and flower swing handle by E., E.J. & W. Barnard. 1832. 13¼ in/33.6 cm diameter. £650–1000.

William III monteith with detachable scalloped rim engraved husk decoration gadrooned cartouches, and lion's mask handles on circular gadrooned foot by Charles Overing. London 1701. 11 in/27.9 cm diameter. £10 000–15 000.

Right Late Victorian monteith with moulded girdle, lobed decoration and spreading lobed foot, the applied rim taken from the early design of above. 1893. 12¾ in/32.5 cm diameter. £900–1200.

Left George I circular punch-bowl with applied wire rim and spreading foot by William Paradise. 1723. 8⅔ in/22 cm. £3000–4500.

Right Victorian rose-bowl with moulded flutes and rococo-style cartouche on moulded decorated foot, chased and embossed by Charles Stuart Harris. 1896. 9⅝ in/24.5 cm diameter. £650–1250.

Dishes and tureens

George II soup tureen and cover with embossed gadroon and foliate decoration with pomegranate finial and cast rococo scroll feet and handles, with engraved armorial by Samuel Courtauld I. 1759. £12 500–15 500.

Pair of George III gadroon edge, sauce tureens on lion mask paw feet, the domed covers with snake handles, crested, by John Edwards III, 1806. £1800–2000.

Soup tureen with gadroon and leaf decoration, heavy cast scroll and foliate handles and applied feet with engraved armorial by John Hunt. 1851. 16 in / 41 cm long. £5000–7000.

A pair of Victorian entrée dishes and covers with gadroon and foliate decoration, removable shell and scroll handles and applied decoration. *c.* 1850. 11¼ in/29 cm long. £2000–3000.

Tankards and mugs

Charles II tankard on spreading circular foot with applied foot rim, single stepped lid, S-scroll handle and bifurcated billet or thumbpiece. London 1664. 7⅛ in / 18 cm high. £5500–7500.

Right George III baluster-shaped tankard with applied reeded girdle, S-scroll handle, domed lid and shell billet or thumbpiece, possibly by John Scofield. 1776. 7½ in / 18.5 cm high. £1500–2000.

William IV christening mug, the campana-shaped body engraved with initials, on a similar decorated pedestal foot, leaf-capped scroll handle, gilt interior, by Charles Fox II, 1834. 4 5/16 in / 11 cm high. £150–200.

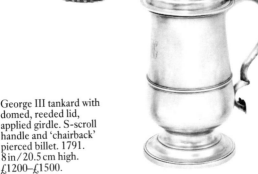

George III tankard with domed, reeded lid, applied girdle. S-scroll handle and 'chairback' pierced billet. 1791. 8 in / 20.5 cm high. £1200–£1500.

156

Tankards and mugs

Queen Anne mug of very simple form with reeded rim and applied reeded foot rim and simple scrolling handle by Thomas Parr I. 1713. 4¼ in / 11 cm high. £500–700.

Left George II mug of baluster form with tuck-in body and applied foot rim, with simple scrolling handle. *c.*1731. 5 in / 13 cm high. £400–500.

George III mug of baluster shape with spreading circular foot and double scroll handle with leaf capping. *c.*1761. 5½ in / 14 cm high. £350–500.

Victorian christening mug with elaborately embossed and chased romantic scene in a floral panel and double scroll handle by Francis Higgins. 1861. £300–400.

Charles I wine goblet with engraved simple armorial and punched date '1639' of slightly tapering shape with cast baluster stem and spreading foot. Maker's mark 'W.R.' London, *c.*1635. 5 in / 12.7 cm high. £3000–5000.

George III goblet with slender stem and beaded circular foot, with bright-engraved decoration of swags and flowers by Walter Brind. 1784. 6½ in / 16.5 cm high. Pairs: £1000–1500. Single: £400–650.

Pair of George III wine goblets of half-fluted baluster form on pedestal circular feet with egg and dart borders, decorated with friezes and cast trailing vines, 5⅞ in / 15 cm high, by Story & Elliott, 1810. Pair: £1000–1200.

Claret and wine jugs

George III vase-shaped ewer with beaded borders, ebonised fruitwood handle, engraved armorial and cast pineapple finial by John Scofield. 1778. 13 in / 32.5 cm high. £950–1450.

Mid-Victorian claret jug with detachable 'stopper'. Engraved with a crest and motto. The 'stopper' flush to the rim, surmounted with a cast finial of grapes and vineleaf, interior gilt, by George Fox, 1867. 9⅞ in / 25 cm high overall. £800–1000.

A pair of Victorian silver-mounted claret jugs with baluster-shaped bodies etched with stars, with embossed and engraved silver mounts, beaded girdle at the base of the neck and bifurcated scroll handles by W. & G. Sissons. Sheffield 1869. Pair £1200–1800.

Late Victorian **plated** claret jugs with mask spouts, embossed mounts decorated with vines and masks on a matted background, with lion finials. c. 1890. Pair: £500–600.

George III wine coasters with pierced sides with Vitruvian scroll decoration and urns by Robert Hennell. 1777. Pair: £1000–1500.

Victorian wine coasters in cast metal in rococo revival style with chased scrollwork and armorial on the bases, by E., E.J. & W. Barnard. 1841. Pair: £1500–1800.

A matched pair of George III coasters, the sides pierced with fruiting vines, one by Benjamin and James Smith, 1811, the other by Benjamin Smith, 1814. 5⅞in/13.7cm diam. £1500–20(

Pair of George IV coasters of unusual design, the shaped circular silver sides finely chased. By Charles Fox II, 1825. 7¹/₁₆in/18cm diameter. £1800–2200.

Wine Labels

a Three Elaborate Bacchanalian wine labels with putti, grapes and vine leaves c.1745. £300–450. **b** Three Victorian wine labels. £200–300. **c** Six Georgian plain wine labels with wavy edges. £500–600. **d** Six Victorian vine-leaf wine labels. £480–550. **e** Five 18th-century Georgian wine labels chased with vine leaves. £250–300.

161

Coffee pots

George II Provincial coffee pot of plain squat, baluster form with scroll embellished spout and acorn finial, engraved with armorials and foliate mantling, by William Partis, Newcastle, 1743. 9⁷/₁₆ in/24 cm high. £1400–1800.

George III baluster coffee pot with decorative knop finial, scalloped spout, scrolled ebonised fruitwood handle with shell mount, possibly by Fuller White 1765. 10½ in/27 cm high. £1200–1600.

Right George III baluster-shaped coffee pot on pedestal foot with high domed lid and acorn finial, cast scrolled animalier spout, scrolled ebonised fruitwood handle with shell and scroll mounts by John Langlands. Newcastle *c.*1790. 10¾ in/27.5 cm high. £1200–1900.

George III coffee pot with gadrooned rim and spreading foot with cast scrolled animalier spout, pineapple finial, domed lid and ebonised fruitwood handle with scroll and shell mounts probably by John Scofield. 1775. 11 in/28.2 cm high. £1800–2200.

Coffee pots

George III urn-shaped coffee pot with beaded borders, high domed lid with urn finial, beaded decoration to the cast applied spout and heavy reeded mounts to the handle by Langlands & Robertson. 1784. 12¾ in / 32 cm high. £1600–2200.

George III coffee biggin with lobed base and decoration with ivory or bone handle by Alice and George Burrows. 1813. 8½ in / 21.5 cm high. £500–700.

Above George III coffee pot on tall pedestal base with thin gadrooned borders and sweeping ebonised handle by William Abdy. 1803. 11¼ in / 28.6 cm high. £600–800.

Left Late Victorian reproduction of side-handled 18th-century coffee pot of 'Queen Anne' style with lidded spout, tapered shape and scrolled billet. 9¾ in / 24.8 cm high. £500–600.

163

George III kettle-on-stand, the hob-shaped kettle with raffia-bound swing handle and small acanthus decoration, the triangular plain stand on flattened paw feet. Lamp marked Wakelin & Taylor. 1782. 14¼ in/36.19 cm high. £1400–1850.

Squat-shaped Victorian kettle-on-stand with chased foliate decoration, flower finial and C-scroll mounts to plain silver handle with ivory collars, the pierced openwork stand with shells and scrolls, on four scrolling feet, by Charles Reilly and George Storer. 1843. £1000–1400.

Flattened pear-shaped tea-kettle with elaborate chased and embossed floral decoration, the animalier spout with mask, C-scroll mounts to silver handle and solid base on scrolled paw feet, by Elkington & Co. 1846. 13 in/33 cm overall. £1600–2400.

Edwardian kettle-on-stand with chased decoration, double scroll mounts to stained ivory handle, the stand pierced and decorated with flowers, on S-scroll and flattened shell feet. By Goldsmiths & Silversmiths Company. c.1909. 13⅜ in/34 cm high. £700–900.

Queen Anne teapot of small capacity with octagonal curved spout cast in two halves and applied, with high-domed lid, stand-away hinge and ebonised handle. 1717. 4½ in/11.5 cm high. £4000–5000.

George II bullet teapot with decorative engraving round the shoulder, flush-fitting lid, cast and applied spout and carved scrolled ivory handle. *c*.1735. 5¼ in/13.5 cm high. £1500–2500.

George III provincial drum-shaped teapot with beaded borders, flush hinge to lid, plain turned finial and ebonised wooden handle. Newcastle 1802. 5¼ in/13.5 cm. £750–1100.

George III oval drum-shaped teapot with bright-cut engraved decoration of floral swags and staved border, with flat stepped lid, flush hinge, plain ebonised finial and sweeping handle, with original reeded stand on small cast feet, by Alexander Field. 1800. Teapot height 5¼ in/13.5 cm. £850–1250.

George III teapot and stand, the body with an upper and lower
bright-cut draped frieze. 7$^{1}/_{16}$ in/18 cm high, the stand with
similar decoration, on four reeded bracket feet, by Peter &
Anne Bateman, 1791. £1200–1400.

William IV teapot with melon-shaped body and lid, on small
scrolling cast shell feet. Profuse floral and leaf decoration to
the body and cast spout and a silver handle which has ivory
collars, by Charles Goodwinor and Charles Gordon. 1832.
6$^{5}/_{8}$ in/17 m high. £400–500.

Victorian teapot of squat
pear-shape with
segmented fluted sides
and domed lid with spiral
finial, diaper and bead
decoration, and silver
handle with ivory collars
by Emes & Barnard.
1862. 6$^{1}/_{4}$ in/16 cm high.
£450–850.

Victorian teapot of melon
shape on leafy scroll feet,
embossed with flowers
and foliate scrolls against
a matted background,
with bud finial and leaf-
capped scroll handles,
7$^{1}/_{4}$ in/18.5 cm high, by
Robert Hennell, 1842.
£450–550.

William IV tea and coffee set in standard popular melon-shape with open-flower finials, and cast decorative feet, the tea and coffee pots both with silver handles and ivory collars, made by different silversmiths and made up from different sets 1815–38. £1250–1750.

Victorian four-piece tea and coffee set in elaborate and popular '*Louis Quatorze*' pattern with rococo cartouche, on small scrolled cast and applied feet, with winged finials by D. & H. Houle. 1857. £1650–2200.

Victorian tea and coffee set of panelled shape on stepped pedestal bases and with engraved swags and oval cartouches and curving spouts, the tea and coffee pots have silver handles with ivory collars, helmet jug and swing handled sugar basket by Elkington & Co. 1873. £1000–1200.

Victorian 'bachelor's' tea set with tapering square sides decorated with Japanese scenes by E. C. Brown. 1876. £750–1000.

Caddy spoons, mote spoons

Victorian die-stamped leaf caddy spoon, the matted bowl chased with veins, the curved handle decorated with scrolls, by Ashforth & Harthorn, Sheffield, 1848. £100–120.

Victorian parcel gilt spoon with handle in the form of coiled stem and lily pad, the bowl as three waterlilies and a rocaille bowl. Birmingham 1856. £140–160.

George IV shovel-shaped bowl with fiddle pattern handle, maker's mark overstruck Richard John Bilton. 1827. £80–100.

Attractive George III strawberry leaf caddy spoon, the matted surface chased with veins, the bifurcated handle with monogrammed oval cartouche, by Joseph Taylor, Birmingham, 1809. £140-160.

Left: George I rat-tailed mote spoon with pierced bowl *c.*1725. £100–170. *Right:* George II gilt mote spoon, the bowl pierced with crosslets and scrolls. *c.*1740. £120–150.

Spoons for collectors

Charles I sealtop spoon
*c.*1640. 7 in / 17.8 cm.
£450–650.

William III trefid spoon
initialled 'MM' London
1698. £250–300.

James I apostle spoon of St.
Matthew, London 1611.
£420–580.

George III bright-cut
spoons, Old English pattern
engraved with contemporary
initials, Hester Bateman
1787. Six £250–300.

Basting spoons and ladles

Above centre George II punch ladle. London 1737. £250–400. *Left* George III Irish gravy spoon, Old English pattern with turn-over end, possibly by Alexander Richards. Dublin 1761. £200–250.
Right Queen Anne basting spoon with rat-tail and egg-shaped bowl 1710. £300–600.

George II basting spoon with turned wood handle by Isaac Cookson. Newcastle 1748. £300–400.

Left George I basting spoon with rat-tail engraved with contemporary initials by Richard Scarlett. London 1722. £275–500. *Right* William IV soup ladle with scalloped bowl and bright-cut decoration. Dublin 1834. £120–210.

Flatware

Above Canteen of late Victorian Old English pattern by George Adams. London 1888. £2000–2800.

Canteen of Victorian and modern mixed makers, Prince's pattern. £2270–3500.

£4000–6000.

Above: Modern canteen of 12 places of rat-tail pattern with bone-handled knives. £2850–3850.

Early Victorian service of fiddle, thread and husk pattern flatware, engraved with a crest, comprising: twelve tablespoons, twelve table forks, twelve dessert spoons, twelve dessert forks, twelve teaspoons, a pair of basting spoons, a set of four sauce ladles, six salt spoons, by

Boxes and vinaigrettes

Top left A late 17th century spice box, of oblong shape with rounded ends, engraved with flowers and with squeeze-action sides, maker's mark only possibly IB. 1¾in/4½cm. *c.* 1680. £400–500.

Centre left An oval Paktong snuff box, the cover decorated in relief with a Topers scene after Tenniers, probably 18th century. £300–400.

Bottom left An early 19th century Russian niello snuff box, with architectural views of Moscow on the cover and base, and similar decoration around the sides, maker's mark FL (Cyrillics). *c.* 1828. £350–450.

Top right An 18th century French boîte-à-mouche, of tortoiseshell lacquered in a plum colour, with gold mounts, the cover applied with an oval enamel plaque of a fruit seller sitting inside her house beside baskets of her produce, the interior with three compartments, two with small hinged covers and set in the cover with a mirror. *c.*1770. £700–800.

Centre right A Russian cloisonné enamel cigarette case, decorated with geometric designs in red, white and four shades of blue, probably by Gustav Klingert, Moscow. *c.*1890. £300–400.

Bottom right An attractive George II gold mounted mocha agate snuff box of cartouche shape chased with flowers. *c.*1745. £700–800.

American vesta case *c.* 1870.
£50–100.

Vesta case with Mr. Punch's
dog *c.* 1890. £80–120.

American vesta case with
Red Indian head *c.* 1880.
£70–100.

Victorian scent bottle shaped
as an owl. £60–80.
18th century scent bottle
with cut star-pattern glass,
open-hinged lid with coronet
and initials. £90–120.

174

Pottery and Porcelain

Introduction by John Sandon

Whenever an auction firm holds an antiques valuation day or experts gather for a 'Roadshow', the pottery and porcelain table always has the longest queues. There is hardly a home which does not have china ornaments decorating its shelves and tea and dinner sets in regular use or condemned to cupboards when out of date. Consequently the number of collectors of ceramics far outnumbers any other sort of antique, and with the vast amount of pottery and porcelain on offer in antiques shops, fairs and auction rooms, there is ample opportunity with always the chance of finding a rarity.

Porcelain has been collected seriously since the 17th century when quantities of Chinese wares were first brought into Europe. This porcelain differed from the European pottery and stoneware in that it was translucent, allowing light to show through it – the crucial difference between porcelain and pottery. During the 18th century fierce competition developed between manufacturers of pottery, striving to improve the quality of their wares, and makers of porcelain attempting to find an economical substitute for imported china.

Early English pottery

Basic handmade traditions which epitomise English Mediaeval pottery developed into country pottery and ultimately the Studio Ceramics of the 20th century. Slipware, crude glazed pottery decorated with different coloured liquid clays or 'slips' rather in the manner of cake icing, was made for ordinary domestic use. The finest dishes by the Toft family and others in the late 17th century are now considered important folk art, selling for £40000 and more, yet it is still possible to buy simple dishes and jugs quite reasonably, especially 19th-century examples.

Stoneware is a high-fired, durable pottery which can be glazed by adding salt to the kiln during the firing. Imported German saltglazed vessels were gradually replaced by English-made domestic wares, the material being refined into superb white saltglazed tearwares from Staffordshire in the mid-18th century. Charming jugs formed as bears are among the most desirable pieces.

In order to imitate Chinese porcelain, the earthenware potters used an opaque white tin glaze applied quite thickly. Named after the town in Holland where the technique was

175

widely used, these delftwares closely resembled the oriental except that they lacked the translucence and delicacy of the originals. Delft was mostly used for making plates and dishes, including deep flanged dishes known as 'chargers'. Other shapes are generally rare and tend to be expensive, while some simple blue and white plates can still be bought for between £40 and £60.

Experiments in Staffordshire in the mid-18th century, particularly by Josiah Wedgwood, perfected a fine quality ivory-coloured earthenware known as creamware, and a blue-tinted variety called pearlware. These could be decorated in many ways, including close copies of Chinese blue and white, and splashed colours underneath the glaze, named after the potter Thomas Whieldon. After a period of development the Staffordshire potters could easily compete with the porcelain makers and the Chinese. Wedgwood also developed a method of colouring fine stoneware clays to produce his famous jasper ware, still popular today after two centuries; likewise a fine black stoneware called 'basalt' was used by Wedgwood and many other factories to produce moulded teawares of exceptional quality which seem considerably undervalued today.

The growth of English porcelain

Enormous demand for Chinese wares and a trade restriction on imported porcelain from Germany and France created a ready market for English-made porcelain. Within a decade from 1745 five principal factories became established, at Chelsea and Bow in London, Longton Hall in Staffordshire, and at Derby and Worcester. In addition there were many smaller makers in Liverpool, Staffordshire and soon afterwards at Lowestoft in East Anglia. All competed for more or less the same market, and each factory soon developed its own versions of the popular Oriental and Continental styles.

The massive popularity of tea drinking in 18th-century England created a great demand for delicate but durable teawares. The Worcester factory's superior porcelain body meant that its teapots did not crack when hot liquid was poured in, a fault which seriously affected most of its competitors. Consequently Worcester had the virtual monopoly for making teapots and collectors find that Worcester's teapots are far more common today than those of any other factory. On the other hand, Worcester figures are exteremely rare, while Derby, Chelsea and Bow, whose bodies were less suited to teawares, produced enormous quantities.

By far the bulk of the production at most factories was blue and white porcelain, directly inspired by Chinese originals although sometimes combining English silver shapes. Transfer-printing introduced at Worcester during the 1750s meant that more elaborate European figure and botanical subjects could be produced more cheaply than by hand painting, a factor which ultimately caused the downfall of many factories, all trying to compete not only with each other but also with the Chinese, and, by the 1780s, with mass produced printed pottery from Staffordshire.

Almost all of the English factories made what is called 'Soft Paste' porcelain which differed in composition and firing conditions from the 'Hard Paste' Chinese porcelain and the wares of the German factories such as Meissen. The materials for making hard paste or 'true' porcelain were not readily available in England, and the only factory making hard paste was at Plymouth, moving to Bristol in 1770. This was not a great success but their hard paste formula was subsequently adapted to make a durable 'hybrid' body at New Hall in Staffordshire where inexpensive teawares directly copied the Chinese exports and sold prolifically alongside the Staffordshire pottery. Many of the pottery makers also turned to making cheaper porcelain services and these undercut considerably the larger established factories of Derby and Worcester. The bigger factories abandoned the cheaper end of the market to Staffordshire where Spode led the way in mass-production of blue-printed services at the beginning of the 19th-century, with designs such as the Willow Pattern supplying a worldwide demand.

The 19th century

At the other extreme, competition was between whichever factory could make the richest and most extravagant service, the highest quality vases and cabinet ornaments and the most elaborate figures. Worcester probably won the battle for the finest wares with Derby close behind, followed by the Welsh factories of Swansea and Nantgarw. Their splendid colours and fine painting typify the Regency period, while humble potters in Stoke-on-Trent made novelties, figures and useful wares for customers with smaller homes and incomes. Generally it is the more expensive products of the time which are the most valuable today, although a great many of the cheaper Staffordshire animals and boldly decorated wares have a primitive charm which is today much sought after, such as the simple dogs and lions, the models of cottages which burned sweet smelling pastilles to disguise the odour of poor sanitation, and the Toby jugs which are as English as can be.

Staffordshire figures represent all aspects of life in Victorian England, and the 'flatbacks', figures modelled on one side only, designed to stand on a mantelpiece, are at their best when they depict well-known personalities of the day. The circus performers and sportsmen stood alongside national heroes of the Crimean War, and the royal families of Europe, simplified to allow the cheapest use of moulds, and gaily painted to cheer up dimly lit homes. There is still great scope for collectors, especially amongst the more simple but delightful studies of children and rustic scenes which can be bought for less than £60.

The Victorian era saw the rise of technology and with it the skills to make almost anything out of clay. It was a period of great exhibitions where manufacturers all tried to outdo each other with the most lavish display and the biggest and greatest vases and fountains. The invention of 'parian', a fine white porcelain left unglazed, meant that copies of marble figures and busts could be made at prices ordinary people could afford. The other great 'invention', although it was really more of a rediscovery, was majolica ware, brightly coloured earthenware with its colours sealed under glaze. This owed its origins more to the Staffordshire wares by Ralph Wood and Whieldon of the previous century than the Italian pottery of the Renaissance after which it was named. Strongly modelled and often of great novelty in design, majolica ware was used for everything from teapots to monumental fountains. These wares by the three biggest makers, Minton, Wedgwood and George Jones, rose dramatically in price after 1982 but it seems to have reached a peak with all but the rarest examples now falling in price.

In the 1870s Japanese art became widely available in England, leading to a 'Japanesque' explosion, seen particularly in the products of Royal Worcester and Minton. Oriental ideals led many manufacturers to break away from the factory processes and experiment with handmade pottery. Henry Doulton wanted individually made 'art pottery' to be available at prices ordinary people could afford and he employed a vast workforce in his Lambeth pottery, making high quality saltglazed stoneware. Technically, Doulton's wares were far ahead of their contemporaries and, because large amounts are available, Doulton has become probably the most collected single factory. Like majolica ware, the better individual pieces are still much sought after while commercial stonewares have not held their value so well.

Twentieth-century trends

The Art Nouveau style did not greatly influence British ceramics but it can be seen in Minton's secessionist ware of the 1900s and Art pottery vases with special glaze effects from potteries such as Ruskin and Moorcroft, while more traditional painted pottery was made at Wemyss near Edinburgh, best known for its models of pigs.

Meanwhile, supplying their more up-market customers, the established porcelain factories continued to produce wares of the highest quality with greater emphasis on fine painting. During the 19th century, artists employed at the factories were rarely allowed to sign their work, but after 1900 a change in attitude, permitting painters to sign, is of great importance to collectors today. The artists working at Royal Worcester are particularly sought after, especially the Stinton family, famed for their highland cattle and game bird subjects, while the Worcester factory continued to produce various ivory effects developed in the 1880s and still very keenly collected. Wedgwood's jasper ware remained as popular as ever, and from the 1910s they produced a range of lustre vases and bowls designed by Daisy Makeig-Jones, adding a new colourful ware to their range. Ordinary lustre pieces by Wedgwood with dragons or butterflies are moderately collectable, while the fantasy designs with elves and pixies, known as 'Fairyland lustre', is the most sought after.

During the 1920s and 1930s the English factories faced extensive competition from cheap imported Chinese and Japanese vases and tea sets as well as traditional pretty figurines and groups from Dresden. Their answer to these were updated designs in the Art Deco style, boldly painted in bright colours by the many young women employed in the Staffordshire potteries. The best known and indeed the most influential designer in the Art Deco style was Clarice Cliff and her name has become synonymous with angular shaped teasets in dramatic colourful patterns or painted with crocuses. Equally influential at the time, although more subtle in her work, was Susie Cooper, the designer of countless dinnerware and teaware patterns.

The role of the designer became ever more important as factories competed for customers in the difficult economic times. Practical, well-designed items that could be produced cheaply kept the manufacturers going during the interwar years and they frequently looked outside the industry to find new designers and modellers. In competition with Dresden figurines, the English factories greatly increased figure production during the 1920s and the market leader was once again Royal Doulton whose wide range of figures and character jugs filled every china shop. Some sold in very large numbers while others proved unpopular and were quickly withdrawn, creating rarities for which certain collectors are today prepared to pay very large sums. The market for Royal Doulton and Royal Worcester figures is subject to considerable fluctuations, with rarity and value going more or less hand in hand. Two figures made in the same year can be of totally different value if one had sold in large numbers while the other had been a failure. It is essential to determine exactly how rare any figure is before any kind of value can be placed on it, and it is worth remembering that prices can come down as well as go up.

After the war, designers played equally important roles in the production of the cheap dinner and tea services and vases in gold, black and white which epitomise the 1950s. Although by no means antique, the better 1950s ceramics have become extremely fashionable again in recent years and are likely to continue their rapid rise in price.

Throughout the 20th century, in contrast to the factory-made products, the Craftsmen Potters movement has become increasingly important. Following traditions established by country potteries since the middle ages, many workshops exist around the country, employing a handful of craftsmen or even just a single potter making wares entirely by hand. Products range from the eccentric grotesque birds made by the Martin Brothers or Edward Bingham's copies of old English slipware made at Castle Heddingham, to sophisticated stonewares and glaze effects by a long list of fine potters headed by Bernard Leach. Leach's work, heavily influenced by the Orient, is already very collectable, as are pots by several of his contempories while a large number of very fine potters have not yet been 'discovered'. Some will certainly prove to be the antique ceramics of the future.

General guides to dating

When present, factory marks are an invaluable guide to collectors, and in many cases are the only means of attributing wares to a particular maker. Earlier painted marks were frequently copied, especially the anchor marks of Chelsea, and should never be taken at face value without other evidence. With very few exceptions, however, any printed mark is likely to be genuine, and can be dated reasonably closely by a good dictionary of marks such as those by Geoffrey Godden or John Cushion and William Honey. It is unfortunate that so little antique porcelain is marked at all. Up until the middle of the 19th century most ceramics were sold by china shops and general dealers who did not encourage manufacturers to mark their wares, preferring that the customers would return to the shop to place additional orders. Only the larger factories, who as a rule had their own retail shops, regularly marked their products.

The most important date to remember is 1891 when, as a

result of the McKinley Tariff Act, items being imported into the United States had to have the name of the country of origin clearly marked on them in English. Most European factories marked all of their products in this way and consequently 'Germany' on a bisque-headed doll, or 'England' incorporated into any mark will mean manufacture after 1891, while 'Made in England' will be after 1900. It should be remembered, however, that the absence of the country of origin does not guarantee a date before 1891, as the McKinley Tariff Act applied only to wares which were likely to be exported to America, and items made exclusively for the home market can be made during this century without the word England. This is particularly true of studio-made pottery and that made by craftsmen.

Registration marks relating to the Patent Office in London can be used to date accurately the year of introduction of a design. From 1842 to 1883 a diamond shaped mark was used with a code system to calculate the year, while after 1884 a registered number record was started, reaching 150000 in 1890, 350000 by 1900 and 550000 by 1910. Once again, a good book of marks will list all of the registration marks and sometimes also the makers.

Many factories used their own system of codes to indicate the date of manufacture. These take the form of printed additions to the factory's backstamp or else numbers or symbols impressed into the clay before glazing. Royal Doulton, Coalport, Copeland and many other of the smaller potteries used the last two numbers of the year. For instance $^6\!/_{89}$ for June 1889 or 3.7.11 for 3 July 1911. Minton and Royal Crown Derby used various geometric shapes and emblems, while Royal Worcester combined symbols with dots. It is necessary to consult a table of date codes in a book of marks for a very accurate dating.

There are certain other generalisations which can be made, such as the word 'Royal' in a factory name will be later than the mid-19th century, while 'bone china' will be 20th century. In the first half of the 19th century, tea and dinner services are very rarely dated but frequently pattern numbers will occur underneath most pieces in a set and these can often be mistaken for a date. Pattern numbers can often be an invaluable clue to attributing wares to a particular factory.

Colour printing was introduced in the 1840s although it was not in general use until the 1880s at least. Fine quality photographic- or litho-printing can easily be mistaken for hand painting and certain care needs to be taken. Through a magnifying glass, colour printing can be made up of tiny dots of colour rather like a photograph in a magazine. Frequently, hand painting can follow a printed outline, and again care needs to be taken. The presence of a signature in no way guarantees that a scene is painted by hand.

Damage and restoration

By its very nature, all porcelain and pottery is fragile and likely to suffer damage, and a large amount of the antique ceramics sold at Phillips is no longer in perfect condition. Most collectors and antique dealers take condition very seriously and even the slightest damage is enough to reduce the value drastically in most cases.

It is somewhat ironic that very rare items will maintain their value better when damaged than common ones. If you can easily find a perfect example why bother with a damaged one; while on the other hand, if the only oportunity for a collector to acquire a great rarity means buying a damaged piece, then it will suffice until the unlikely event of a perfect one being available to replace it. A true collector will never turn down the chance of adding a desirable piece to a collection just because of damage, as long as the price charged correctly reflects the damage. A collection can always be upgraded as better examples become available.

Having said this, damage must always be taken into account, and there are no easy rules to help calculate the loss in value. Generally speaking, the slightest damage such as a hairline crack or a small chip will account for at least half of the price, rising to 90 per cent or more for very serious damage, but this does not apply in all cases. Some materials such as delftware are so soft that chipping is almost inevitable, with the result that chips to the rim of a delft plate would make no significant difference to the value, while a chip to a Royal Worcester plate or rare Doulton figure would be considered as extremely serious.

Nowadays restoration can be so advanced that even extensive damage can be disguised. It is worth remembering, though, that this is all it does and even the most expensive repair cannot make a piece perfect again. It is purely cosmetic and in the case of disfiguring damage it is very worthwhile, as nothing looks worse than a figure with a broken head or a teapot missing its spout. Repair that puts back the missing part so that it is visually attractive will add to the value, but restoration can be taken too far. Collectors of early pottery and porcelain prefer to see an honest crack, perhaps simply cleaned and touched up, while large areas of spray in order to pretend that the piece is perfect, is definitely offputting. Good restoration is expensive, and care must be taken in deciding the value of the piece both before and after repair, as some repairs can cost more than the value of the item in perfect condition.

Because good repairs can only be detected by an experienced eye, it is best to buy only from a reputable auction house which mentions restoration in their catalogue, or from a dealer who is prepared to give a written receipt stating the condition and guaranteeing that there is no hidden damage. Any dealer unwilling to give such a receipt should not be trusted.

Late 17th-century English delft 'blue dash' charger with lead-glazed back, decorated in green, blue, orange and yellow. 13⅜ in/34 cm diameter. £1500–2000.

Left London delft ovoid drug jar, painted in blue with an elaborate scroll cartouche with shell above and angel head below, flanked by two winged putti holding flowers, inscribed 'U:Cærul: Mit:' ('The blue ointment' used as an anti-venereal agent). 7¼ in/18.5 cm. £300–500.

Right English delft ovoid drug jar, painted in blue with an angel head and shell cartouche flanked by putti inscribed 'C:Nymphæ' (white water lily). 7¹⁄₁₆ in/ 18 cm. £300–350.

Pair of English delft drug jars, of ovoid shape, title 'U. Ægyptiac' and 'C. Paulin' within blue cartouches painted with birds, leaves, flowers, scrolls and a winged cupid head. 15½ in/14 cm. (Aegyptiac was an Egyptian ointment.) £300–400.

Delft

Documentary Liverpool delft ship bowl, the centre painted in
blue, green and red with a two-masted brig, inscribed 'Success
to the Indeavour (sic), Capt. Littledale', the exterior painted
with a chinoiserie landscape with figures in blue. 10⅝in/
27 cm. £600–700.

Liverpool delft bowl with 'Fazakerley' style decoration in
yellow, blue and manganese with green leaves.
9⅞in/25 cm diameter *c.*1750. £1000–1200.

Delft 'blue and white'

English delft tea caddy with blue and white 'chinoiserie' decoration of flowers and foliage with birds, and Jacob and Rebecca at the Well. 3⅞in/9.7cm. *c.*1720. £1500–2000.

Left English delft dish with everted rim decorated in blue and white with a Chinese scene. 13¾in/35cm diameter. Early 18th century. £300–500.

Right English or Dutch delft dish *c.*1700 decorated with a fox and goose chase, painted in blue with 'sponged' trees. £1000–1500.

London delft plate of Admiral Keppel with iron red rim and manganese inscription, the portrait in blue and white style. 8⅞in/22.7cm diameter. £500–700.

ADMIRAL KEPPEL FOR EVER.

Lowestoft butter pot in moulded salt-glaze with fluted body and lid, and red borders. (1760–65). £400–600.

Staffordshire salt-glaze teapot with crabstock handle and enamelled decoration of a white rose and thistle with portrait of Charles Edward Stuart, probably later decoration. *c.*1750. 5½in/14cm high. £600–800.

Rare early teapot painted in polychrome colours of red, blue, green and yellow. 5⅜in/13.5cm. £700–900.

Salt-glazed stoneware

Staffordshire white salt-glazed jar and cover formed as a bear with details in brown slip, second quarter of the 18th century. 8½ in / 21.5 cm high. £6000–7500.

English brown stoneware jug, probably London, dated 1767. £500–700.

German 17th century salt-glazed bellarmine with stamped relief decoration of medallions on body and with bearded mask on neck. 14⅛ in / 36 cm. £300–400.

Whieldon teapot of globular shape with moulded fruiting vine decoration and crabstock handle, streaked with green, grey and manganese glaze *c.*1760. 4⅜ in/11 cm high. £1000–1300.

Wedgwood/Whieldon melon-shaped teapot with applied moulded leaf and flower decoration with leaf and stem handle, engine-turned with dots in 'egg and spinach' colours *c.*1760–65. £2500–3500.

187

English porcelain teapots

Left Christian Liverpool teapot with strap handle and moulded fluted body decorated with scroll-edged panels with red scroll border. 6⅞ in / 17.5 cm *c*.1765. £400–600.

Centre Worcester teapot with Chinese decoration of figures in panels outlined in puce with gilt scrolls. First period *c*.1765. 5¾ in / 14.5 cm. £700–1000.

Right Lowestoft teapot of globular shape painted in green enamel outlined in black. Cypher mark 'AA'. 6½ in / 16.5 cm. £600–800.

Worcester teapot of fluted barrel shape with flower finial decorated with butterflies and birds in panels edged with gold rococo scrolls, with blue scale ground. First period *c*.1765–70. 5⅞ in / 15 cm. £1000–1500.

Early teapot shapes

Worcester teapot of round globular shape with flower finial decorated with butterflies and birds in panels edged with gold rococo scrolls, with blue scale ground. First period *c.*1765–68. 5⅞ in/15 cm. £1500–2000.

Above left Worcester barrel-shaped teapot with flower finial with sprays of flowers in panels edged with gold scrolls, on apple green ground. *c.*1770. 5½ in/14 cm high. £1500–2500.
Above right Round globular-shaped teapot with flower finial decorated with garlands and insects, with flower finial and pale turquoise ground. *c.*1775. 5⅞ in/15 cm high. £300–500.

Worcester teapot with 'hop trellis' pattern with fluted barrel-shaped body decorated with green garlands, gold scrolls and puce herringbone border. *c.*1770–75. 5⅛ in/13 cm high. £2000–3000.

189

Left Longton Hall coffee can decorated in underglaze blue with 'Folly' pattern *c.*1775. £1500–1800. *Right* Bow miniature teapot with underglaze blue decoration of trailing vines. *c.*1765. 3¾ in/9.5 cm high. £800–1000.

Above Liverpool 'Chaffers' octagonal soup plate painted with a Chinese landscape. *c.*1757. £600–800.

Early Worcester jug with enamelled decoration of Chinese scene, with pear-shaped body and plain spout. *c.*1755. £1200–1400.

Worcester blue and white coffee can with 'prunus fence' pattern *c.*1756. £1000–1200.

Lowestoft miniature tea service in blue and white decorated with Chinese river scenes. £1200–1800.

Silver shapes

Early Worcester sauceboat of silver shape with moulded scroll decoration and 'famille rose' coloured enamels. c.1753–55. 6¼in/16 cm. £1200–1500.

Worcester two-handled sauceboat with scallop moulded lip c.1756–58. 7⅜in/18.7 cm. £800–1000.

Worcester rococo sauceboat with raised wavy-edged sides. c.1755. 7⅝in/19.3 cm. £600–900.

Early Worcester pickle dish in 'famille rose' coloured enamels and fluted shell shape. c.1753–55. 4⅝in/11.7 cm. £800–1200.

Worcester sauceboat with 'famille rose' decoration in enamels
with scroll handle *c.*1753. 6½ in / 16.5 cm. £1500–2000.

Worcester sauceboat with gadroon moulding picked out in
puce with puce scrollwork, painted in colours, with moulded
fluted body. First period *c.*1760. 5⅞ in / 15 cm. £600–1000.

Chelsea plate moulded in rococo silver shape with panels of
flowers painted in colours. Red anchor period 1752–56.
9 in / 23 cm diameter. £1500–1800.

193

Leaf shapes

Chelsea peony flower dish with leaf and stem handle. Red anchor period 1752–56. 9 in/23 cm. £2000–2500.

Below Bow leaf sauceboat with puce ribbing to stem handle and green and yellow decoration. c.1760. £800–1000.

Large Worcester cabbage leaf jug with double 'C'-scroll handle, painted in underglaze blue with a floral design of a flowering tree, birds and insects, (I.E.21). Pseudo-Meissen crossed swords mark, c.1755–60. 10¼ in/26 cm. £600–700.

Chelsea acanthus moulded coffee cup and saucer with moulded leaf pattern and rococo handle. Red anchor period 1752–56. 3⅛ in/8 cm height. £1000–1200.

Worcester coffee cup and saucer printed in lilac with classical
landscape scenes with enamelled and gold decoration. First
period *c.*1775. £600–800.

Left Liverpool creamware
ship bowl inscribed
'Succefs to the Thomas
and Sally' printed black
outside with centre
painted in colours *c.*1786.
£1500–2000.

Above Rare Bow transfer-
print plate with borders in
grey-black and centre in lilac
with 'St. George' and 'For
our Country' probably by
Robert Hancock. 9 in / 23 cm
diameter. *c.*1755. £1000–1500.

Worcester tankard printed in
black by Robert Hancock
with half-length portrait of
William Pitt flanked by
'Fame' and 'Minerva'.
*c.*1761. 5¾ in / 14.7 cm.
£2000–2500.

195

Printed and transfer wares

Windsor Castle: a large serving dish with a beaded rim, possibly Ralph Stevenson, from the British Palaces series, the central scene within a very elaborate lace and floral border. Printed British Palaces mark. 1 ft 10 in/56.5 cm. £150–200.

Left Bisham Abbey: a spill vase, possibly Davenport, the Tudor mansion set among exotic looking trees, unusual floral border. 5⅜ in/13.7 cm. £60–80.

Right Grazing rabbits: a fine large cylindrical mug, the three rabbits in a panoramic landscape, a floral border inside. 5¼ in/13 cm. Possibly James Keeling. £250–300.

Left The cowman: a plate with a rustic scene featuring a thatched cottage and single large cow, within a floral border. 9⅞ in/25 cm. £80–100.

Right Crystal Palace: a J. and M. P. Bell soup plate depicting the exhibition building in Hyde Park, the border with Windsor Castle, Westminster Abbey and St. Paul's Cathedral. 10¼ in/26 cm. Printed mark. £70–90.

196

Chelsea octagonal tea bowls decorated with flower sprigs. Red anchor mark and period 1753–56. 2⅜ in and 2¾ in / 6 cm and 7 cm height. £600–800.

Chelsea bell-shaped coffee cup and 'trembleuse' saucer. Red anchor mark 1753–56. £600–800.

Longton Hall octagonal tea bowl and saucer painted in imitation Chelsea style. Middle period 1749–60. £800–900.

Tea bowls and cups

Worcester coffee cup and saucer of fluted form with deep blue
border and four gilt diaper bands, on turquoise ground. First
period 'W' in blue. c.1770. £1200–1500.

Chelsea tea bowl and 'trembleuse' saucer painted with sprays
of flowers. Red anchor period 1752–56. £500–700.

Chelsea octagonal tea bowl decorated in green, red and blue
enamels with the 'lady and pavilion' Kakiemon pattern. Raised
anchor period c.1750. £1500–2500.

Right Worcester tea bowl
decorated in finely pencilled
black. First period *c.* 1755–83.
£800–1000.

Far right Chelsea tea bowl
and saucer finely painted
with birds and butterflies
with a ladybird painted on
the interior of the bowl. Red
anchor mark 1753–56.
£600–800.

199

Worcester leaf dish with twig handle in brown and yellow, black veining on leaf and small moulded snail. Pierced for hanging. First period *c.*1760. 9 in / 23 cm. £600–800.

Worcester dessert dish of lobed oval shape, with deep wet-blue ground and gilt and enamel decoration. First period *c.*1770. 9⅜ in / 24 cm. £400–600.

Worcester lobed dessert dish with deep wet blue border and scalloped shape, decorated with garlands and an exotic bird. *c.*1775. £600–800.

Worchester scallop rimmed plate en suite. £400–600.

Right Worcester plate with wavy edge decorated with two exotic birds on branches. *c.*1770. 8⅞ in / 22.5 cm. £600–800.

Embossed Chelsea plate after a Meissen pattern, decorated with painted butterflies, with the rim edged in brown. Red anchor mark 1752–56. 9⅜ in / 23.7 cm. £800–1000.

18th-century patterns and shapes

Worcester dessert centre dish with osier moulded border, raised on foot, with decorated underside and centre painted with fabulous birds. First period c.1765–70. £1500–1800.

Worcester Blind Earl plate. c.1770. 7⁷⁄₁₆in/19 cm. £600–800.

Swansea shell-shaped dessert dish decorated with trailing vines in brown and gold and painted in sepia monochrome inscribed 'Marino, a Casino belonging to the Earl of Charlemont' by William Weston Young. Impressed Swansea. 8¼in/21 cm. £800–1000.

'Japan patterns'

Worcester fan-pattern dessert dish with Japan-style decoration with central gilt mons, half mons in blue, red, green and gold, with blue inner border. Pseudo character mark. First period. *c.*1765–70. 7½in/19cm. £600–800.

Worcester dessert dish decorated in red, blue, pink and green with deep blue divisions in the 'Japan' style. Flight & Barr period, incised 'B' mark. *c.*1805. £600–800.

Left Worcester dessert dish with underglaze blue, painted in Japan colours, with pseudo Chinese marks. First period *c.*1770. £650–850. *Right* Worcester chocolate cup and saucer of ogee form with lamprey handles and 'Old Mosaic' pattern decorated in underglaze blue with 'Japan' colours. First period *c.*1770. £700–900.

Heart-shaped dessert dish painted in blue with the Kang Hsi Lotus pattern (I.F.3). Mark of an oriental emblem *c.*1770. 10¼in/26cm. £500–700.

Chestnut warmers, tureens

Worcester moulded partridge tureens with chestnut brown decoration *c.*1756–58. 6⅛ in / 15.5 cm. Pair: £2000–4000.

Longton Hall cos lettuce tureen with leaves edged in lettuce green and interior painted with leaves and flowers to hide kiln imperfections. Sprouting bud finial. *c.*1775. £2500–3000.

Derby chestnut basket with honeycomb moulded body and pierced lid and dish with applied twig and leaf handles, painted in blue with cruciform flowers and Chinese river landscapes. 8 in / 20 cm across. £1000–1500.

Derby chestnut basket with rope-twist finial, trellis-moulded body and cover, with pierced cover and applied flower decoration, painted with moths and cherries. Basket 8½ in / 21.5 cm, dish 8¼ in / 21 cm diameter. £600–800.

Liverpool 'Chaffers' creamware mug with strap handle and bell-shaped body, decorated with a dove and olive branch. *c.*1760. £2000–3000.

Bow tankard of bell shape with curved strap handle painted in colours with garlands and flowers and a ladybird, the inside rim decorated with puce spirals. *c.*1755–60. 3¼in/9.5cm. £700–900.

Worcester cylindrical tankard with deep blue scale ground, gold rococo scrolls and fabulous birds painted in colours. First period *c.*1770. 5⅞in/15cm. £1200–1500.

Pinxton porter mug, engine-turned with chequer pattern, and a border of pink roses on a black ground with gold bands. Late 18th century. 5⅜in/13.5cm. £200–300.

Jugs

New Hall presentation jug decorated with peonies and roses, a gilt Greek key neckband and a gilt monogram 'TG'. c.1785. 7½ in/19 cm. £800–1200.

Above Worcester blue-scale cabbage-leaf jug with mask spout and ring handle decorated with scrolling rococo gold-outlined panels with flowers. 5⅞ in/23 cm. c.1770. £1200–1500.

Above left Worcester cabbage-leaf mask jug with ring handle and printed decoration of flowers and trailing vines. First period c.1765. 9 in/23 cm. £400–600.

Above right Early New Hall type jug with moulded overlapping cabbage leaves with puce leaf and red star motifs, edged with blue enamel. 5½ in/14 cm. c.1790. £400–600.

Right Bristol hard-paste jug with mask spout, painted in colours with sprigs of flowers. £600–800.

Tea services

New Hall bone china tea and coffee set with coffee cans and tea cups printed with fruit, with gilded rims. c.1815. £2000–2500 (45 pieces).

A New Hall style tea set decorated in yellow and gold with 12 tea bowls and coffee cups, in hybrid hard-paste porcelain. c.1790. £800–1200.

Tea services

Caughley tea service with vertical flutes, decorated by Chamberlain of Worcester in gilt with blue enamel berries. £2000–2500.

New Hall tea and coffee service decorated with pattern no. 446 of a gilt outlined blue tree with orange berries and gilt 'seaweed' foliage, comprising: a teapot and cover, sucrier and cover, jug, one cake plate, three coffee cans, six cups and four saucers. Pattern no. 446. £500–600.

Tea services

Derby tea service in 'Smith's blue' with gilt cartouche, painted with landscapes surrounded with blue enamel bands. c.1785. £3000–3500 (45 pieces).

Spode tea set decorated with cabbage rose pattern no. 2812. c.1815. £1500–2000 (45 pieces).

Spode tea set decorated with a 'Japan' pattern border. c.1815. £2000–2500 (45 pieces).

Belleek 'spiders' web' tea set wtih twig handles and scalloped rims, with two cups and saucers. Late 19th century. £1000–1500.

Early Coalport tea service, painted in rich Japan style with the so-called 'Finger and Thumb' pattern, comprising: a teapot, cover and stand, sucrier and cover, bowl, jug, two cake plates, eight teacups, four coffee cans and ten saucers. £700–900.

209

Above Spode dessert service derived from silver shapes, painted in 'Japan' colours. *c.*1815. £1500–2000 (27 pieces).

Below Pearlware dessert service boldly painted with ornithological pattern with gilt line borders. £1200–1500 (31 pieces).

Dessert services

Caughley dessert service in underglaze blue with a formal flower pattern and gilded borders, in lobed and fluted shapes. 45 pieces including a pair of ice pails. c.1790. £3000–4000.

Derby dessert service with lime green borders and formal gilded borders, painted with landscapes. 36 pieces including pairs of tureens and ice pails. c.1800. £6000–8000.

Dessert services

Coalport dessert service with deep blue borders and rococo gilded scrollwork painted with wild birds with gilt beaded borders. Mock Sèvres marks enclosing 'R'. £1000–1200.

Davenport dessert service with pink borders and gilded scrollwork, painted with landscapes, with printed marks 'Davenport, Longport, Staffordshire'. £2000–3000 (18 pieces).

Dessert services

Rare Wedgwood bone china dessert service with a matt jet black ground and puce leaves. Marked 'Wedgwood' in red. Pattern no. 686. *c.*1815. £2500–3500 (32 pieces).

Minton dessert service, boldly decorated in colours in the Aesthetic style with different fruits on flowering branches, with cream backgrounds, including oranges, gooseberries and redcurrants amongst others, the rims gold, comprising: two high comports, four low comports and eleven plates, impressed Mintons, date marks for 1876 and 1878, pattern no. G 3000. 9⁷⁄₁₆in/24cm. £600–800.

Dessert plates

Royal Worcester dessert plate with claret ground borders finely decorated with gilt tracery and gilt borders. Signed A. Shuck. 1925. £200–250.

Right Royal Worcester dessert plate with deep blue borders decorated with gilt rococo husks, swags and scrolls, the centres filled with fruit. Signed R. Sebright. 1926.
9 in/23 cm diameter.
£400–600.

Left Royal Worcester dessert plate by Richard Sebright with deep blue and pale pink panelled grounds with raised gold and scroll border. 1917.
8⅝ in/22 cm diameter.
£300–500.

Royal Worcester dessert plate with deep blue ground and gold sprays, painted with landscape by G. Johnson. Date code for 1909.
£200–300.

Rockingham miniature teapot in the Dresden manner with applied flowers, decorated in gilt with green twig handle. Griffin mark in red. 2½in/6.5cm. *c.*1828–30. £400–600.

Cabinet cup and stand, possibly Welsh, with 'biting snake' handle, a pale primrose yellow ground with wide gold border band, of similar shape to Swansea. *c.*1818. £300–500.

Ecuelle and cover flanked by two cups and stands with handles of 'eagle and lamprey in combat', decorated with bands of simulated pearls, bordered with white and gilt with seaweed pattern. Barr, Flight & Barr. 7¾in/19.5cm. *c.*1810. Cups £600–800 each. Ecuelle £1000–1400.

Garnitures

Spode spill vases in bright 'Japan' colours with beaded rims,
marked in red SPODE 967. 6¼ in and 4⅜ in / 16 cm and 11 cm.
*c.*1820. £1200–1500.

Minton 'pate-sur-pate' vases with decoration of elves and
fairies on a deep slate-blue ground and gilt borders with 'Dog
of Fo' handles. 1890. 16⅛ in / 41 cm. £4000–5000 pair.

216

Bloor Derby garniture of classical urn shape with scrolling leaf-capped handles with dark blue ground and gilt decoration. 11¼ in and 8⅞ in / 28.5 cm and 22.5 cm. *c.*1830. £1500–2000.

Royal Worcester garniture with pierced necks and scroll feet in bronze and gold, painted with Highland cattle by Harry Stinton. Date code for 1911. £1700–2000.

217

Pair of Bow Putti candlestick figures, on turquoise and gilt pierced bases, surmounted by candle nozzles and drip-guards decorated with flowers and scrolls in blue and gilding, anchor and dagger marks in red. 8⅝ in/ 22 cm. £800–1000.

A pair of Coalbrookdale candlesticks edged in green and gilt with painted flower panels with applied flowerheads on rococo bases. 9⅝ in/24.5 cm. *c.*1830. £1000–1200.

Minton table centrepiece with heavily gilt dolphin columns supporting three shells on the lower tier applied with flowers, with basket of coloured flowers above. *c.*1830–35. £1000–1400.

Minton bowl with scrolled gilt feet heaped with flower heads and berries, in full relief. Pseudo Meissen crossed swords mark. 10⅝in/27cm. *c.*1830. £1200–1500.

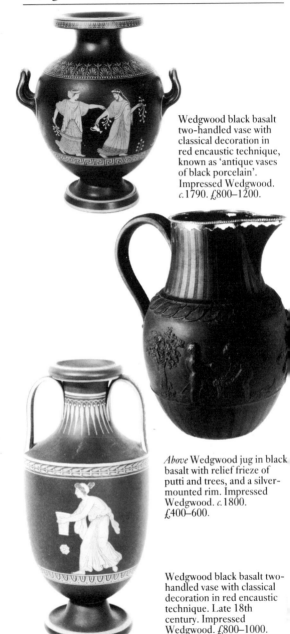

Wedgwood black basalt two-handled vase with classical decoration in red encaustic technique, known as 'antique vases of black porcelain'. Impressed Wedgwood. *c.*1790. £800–1200.

Above Wedgwood jug in black basalt with relief frieze of putti and trees, and a silver-mounted rim. Impressed Wedgwood. *c.*1800. £400–600.

Wedgwood black basalt two-handled vase with classical decoration in red encaustic technique. Late 18th century. Impressed Wedgwood. £800–1000.

Wedgwood jasper ware

Wedgwood cabinet coffee can and saucer in 'Trophy' pattern with black jasper dip ground and applied decoration in white, of rams' heads, swags and garlands. Impressed Wedgwood. Early 19th century. £500–700.

Wedgwood three-colour jasper coffee can and saucer of mosaic-type pattern with vertical flower and leaf bands. Early 19th century. £600–800.

Wedgwood blue jasper dip teapot with scenes of 'Domestic Employment' in white relief, with fluted base. Impressed Wedgwood. 4¾in/12 cm. Late 18th century. £600–800.

Above Green jasper dip cream jug with acanthus lip and putti in white relief with fluted base. Impressed Wedgwood. 2⅞in/7.5 cm. *c.*1820. £250–350.

Wedgwood green jasper dip Portland vase with loop handles with bearded mask terminals and decoration in applied white relief, with a classical half-length portrait on the base. Impressed Wedgwood. 10⅝in/27 cm high. Early 19th century. £1500–2000.

Wedgwood blue jasper dip butter dish with putti and acanthus leaves in white relief. Impressed Wedgwood in lower case mark. 6⅝in/17 cm diameter. *c.*1785. £600–800.

Wedgwood 'Fairyland lustre'

Above Wedgwood fairyland lustre bowl, decorated on the interior with the 'Jumping Faun' design of little folk and fairies amongst trees, foliage and waterscapes, the exterior with the 'Feather Hat' variation of the 'Woodland Elves' pattern, with well-defined gilt spiders' webs. 10$\frac{1}{16}$ in/25.5 cm. £600–800.

Right Vase bordered with fish on a light green ground with 'Firbolgs' and 'Thumbelina' fairies in black and gold on claret ground. 8$\frac{7}{8}$ in/22.5 cm diameter. £1000–1200.

Wedgwood fairyland lustre footed bowl, the exterior decorated with 'Poplar Trees' pattern and the interior with the 'Woodland Bridge' pattern with bridges, trees, fairies, birds and a central mermaid, Portland Vase mark, pattern no. Z4968. 11 in/28 cm. £700–900.

19th-century vases and decorative ware

Doulton Lambeth oviform vases decorated by Eliza Banks in white, brown and green with 'pate-sur-pate' technique. 1883. 12¼in/31·5 cm. £400–600.

Examples of Moorcroft pottery with typical tube-line decoration. *Left* A 'Hazeldene' vase. 5 in/17½ cm. £800–1000. *Right* A Moorcroft Macintyre vase. £600–800.

Above Selection of Wemyss pottery. *Left* Pig with shamrock, marked Wemyss. 17 in/50 cm. £6000–8000. *Right* pig marked 'Wemyss Made in England'. £4000–5000. *Above* Duck flower holder. £500–800.

Right Royal Worcester vase and cover, painted with fruit, signed Ricketts. Date code for 1925. 10 in/25.5 cm. £1200–1500.

Left Moorcroft Macintyre 'Florian ware' vase of double gourd shape with olive-coloured leaves on a white ground. 6⁷/₈ in/17.5 cm. £800–1000.

Royal Worcester ewer, painted with swans in flight, with gilt acanthus leaf moulding and high scrolled leaf-capped handle. Signed C. Baldwyn. Shape no. 1309. Date code for 1907. 15⅜ in/39 cm. £3000–4000.

Royal Worcester pot pourri vase and cover, painted with sheep in a landscape with simulated basket-weave base and pierced cover. Signed H. Davis. Date code for 1925. 11⅞ in/30 cm. £2000–2500.

19th-century vases and decorative wear

English porcelain pot pourri vase and cover of elaborate squared baluster shape moulded and pierced with gilt rococo scrollwork on a rose pink ground, the reserved arched panels painted with colourful flowers against shaded backgrounds, modelled nosegay finials. 14³/₁₆ in/ 36 cm. Pair: £600–800.

Pair of Barr, Flight and Barr vases of simple trumpet shape on circular bases, painted with spiral festoons of pink roses against a marbled grey ground, impressed BFB and crown marks. 3¹/₈ in/8 cm. £600–800.

Left Spode two-handled vase on circular foot painted in Imari palette with panels of flowers on a blue and gilded ground, pattern no. 1216, marked in red. 6⁵/₁₆ in/ 16 cm. £300–500.

Right Spode trumpet-shaped vase with a gilt bordered shell-shaped panel well-painted with a flower composition, reserved on a rich blue ground gilt with foliage and painted on the reverse with a daffodil and convolvulus, pattern no. 2575, marked Spode. 6¹/₈ in/ 15.5 cm. £300–400.

'Martha Gunn' Brighton bathing woman with gin bottle and Prince of Wales feathers in her hat. 10¼ in / 26 cm. £1200–1500.
Right Toby jug possibly by Ralph Wood Jnr. Staffordshire, with pale blue coat and puce breeches 10⅜ in / 26.3 cm. £550–800.
Below Ralph Wood Toby jug with olive coat and green waistcoat. *c.*1780. 10 in / 25.3 cm. £1200–1500.

Lord Rodney, possibly by Ralph Wood Jnr., related to the Derby series of admirals by Stephan. 12½ in / 32 cm. £1000–1200.

Below Toby jug of Ralph Wood type with light brown coat and yellow breeches. 10⅛ in / 25.8 cm. £600–800.

Staffordshire & Royal Worcester figures

Staffordshire figure of a Turk wearing a brown coat, black fez and yellow turban and standing on a square base. 5⁵⁄₁₆in/13.5 cm. £180–200.

A very rare figure of 'Ripe 'Speragas' from the London Cries series, the lady holding a shallow basket under one arm and further asparagus gathered in her orange apron, shape no. 3250, script mark, date code for 1941. By Gwendoline Parnell. 5⁷⁄₈in/15 cm. £300–500.

An impressive group of 'The Planter's Daughter' modelled in Cheyne Chelsea style as a young lady seated, the servant at her feet, shape no. 3138, puce title and date code for 1936, impressed modeller's mark. By Gwendoline Parnell. 9¹⁄₁₆in/23 cm. £300–400.

A group of 'Young Fox-hounds', the three puppies seated together and finely painted, shape no. 3132, black mark with no date code, 1943–1949. By Doris Lindner. 3¼in/8.2 cm wide. £300–400.

Staffordshire pottery figures

Whieldon type lion splashed and sponged in manganese, cobalt and ochre on a green base. 3⅛ in/8 cm high. *c.*1770. £500–800.

Whieldon type lion splashed only in manganese. 2¾ in/7 cm. Late 18th century. £400–600.

Staffordshire lion with ochre spots and manganese mane. 2¾ in/7 cm. Pratt type. *c.*1790. £300–500.

Staffordshire lamb on modelled base, sponged with orange. 2¾ in/7 cm. *c.*1800. £150–200.

Staffordshire lamb sponged with orange and black. 2⅜ in/6 cm. £50–100.

230

Early Staffordshire cow creamer and a replacement cover, the cream coloured body streaked in dark brown and standing on a flat green glazed base. 5⁵⁄₁₆in/13.5 cm. £600–800.

Cow creamer and cover sponged in black and puce standing, with its back legs tied, on a flat green sponged base with a figure of a milkmaid. 5⁵⁄₁₆in/13.5 cm. £400–600.

Alert Staffordshire cow creamer and a cover, the animal sponged in yellow ochre and dark brown with brown horns, standing on a stepped base sponged in blue and applied with a milkmaid. 5¹¹⁄₁₆in/14.5 cm. £400–500.

Pastille burners

Yorkshire pottery two-storey moneybox with male and female standing figures, blue roof, orange and green decoration and children at the upper windows. 4½ in/11.5 cm. Early 19th century. £300–400.

Lighthouse encrusted with moss with pierced slit windows. *c.*1840. £400–600.

Above Octagonal pavilion encrusted with vegetation with pierced slits. 3⅜ in/8.5 cm. £180–220.

Staffordshire pottery pastille burner with green vegetation. 3½ in/9 cm. *c.*1830. £200–300.

Pastille burners

Chamberlain Worcester pastille burner in biscuit porcelain incised 'Chamberlain's Royal Porcelain Worcester'.
5½ in/14 cm.
£800–1000.

Left Pastille burner with Gothic windows on separate base.
5½ in/14 cm. *c.* 1835.
£200–300.

Pastille burner of Gothic folly with columns and twisting chimney.
5⅝ in/14.5 cm.
c. 1835. £300–400.

Pastille burner with applied coloured flowers.
5½ in/14 cm. *c.* 1840.
£200–250.

Twentieth century

Above Wedgwood service of Travel pattern, designed by Eric Ravilious, printed in black and light blue. Early 1950s. Price range £20–30 small jug; £50–80 large dish.

Above Group of 20th century studio pottery. Leaping salmon vase by Bernard Leach. £800–1000. Beaker by Bernard Leach. £250–350. Bowl by Charles Vyse. £150–200. Dish by Michael Cardew. £150–200. Vase by Michael Cardew. £80–100.

Right Pilkington 'Royal Lancastrian' vase by Gordon Forsyth. 1908. £400–600.

Above & above right Doulton stonewares decorated with animal subjects by Hannah Barlow. 1874–1903. Vase (*right*) 12 in/31.5 cm. £600–800. *Left* £200–500.

Right Royal Doulton whisky flask in 'Kingsware' made for Dewar's Scotch Whisky. Churchwarden pattern. 9 in/24.5 cm. Early 20th century. £300–400.

Below John Barleycorn character jug modelled by C. J. Noke 1934. Rare factory mark. £200–300.

Thirties pottery

Above left Dish by Charlotte
Rheed in Bursley ware.
Signed. *c.*1930. £250–350.
Right Shallow bowl with Art
Deco design by Clarice Cliff.
Newport pottery mark.
*c.*1930. £400–600.

Right Wedgwood plate
painted by E. Lessore
with moulded lobed
border. Impressed
Wedgwood.
9³⁄₈in/24cm. £100–120.

Ruskin pottery jug covered
with rich red, purple and
green 'high fired' glaze.
Impressed Ruskin and dated
1933. £300–400.

Glass

In contrast to almost every other field of antique buying and collecting, the field of English glass has not kept pace with rapidly rising prices, and today it could be said that it is undervalued in comparison with other sections of the market. There are many explanations for this, but none of them are very satisfactory. In all probability glass remains the least-favoured field because people find it rather cold and impersonal, and it needs to be well displayed to be properly appreciated. There is also a general feeling that it is too breakable to use and enjoy, and too fragile to spend much money on. This is understandable but curious, because the amount of glass which has survived from the 18th century onwards should be proof enough that, on the contrary, it is remarkably tough and enduring.

On the other hand, a whole new field has opened up over the past few years in buying and collecting 19th- and even 20th-century glass, of a kind which for years has been dismissed as unimportant, bad taste, or just plain old-fashioned. The interest in glass as a decorative material was revived in the 19th century, with new and rediscovered processes and techniques of staining, colouring, overlaying and flashing, as well as reproducing the ancient and grand 'façon de Venise' glass of 16th-century Italy. These highly decorative pieces have attracted a following of new collectors who have little interest in the more purist, aesthetic appreciation of English 18th-century glass. Both are still relatively small collecting fields, and of the two it is 19th- and 20th-century glass which today commands the higher price.

English glass

The history of English glass begins in about 1670 when George Ravenscroft obtained a licence to produce a new formula glass called 'flint glass' or 'glass of lead'. Until then the monopoly for making and supplying glass to England had been held by the Venetians, whose glass was made to a different formula, seldom brilliantly clear and often with a pale straw-coloured or greenish tinge. Until his licence expired, only Ravenscroft's glass houses at Henley-on-Thames and in London produced his new formula glass, but as soon as they were able, glass houses all over England began to make 'glass of lead' to Ravenscroft's formula.

As with pottery and porcelain, glass-making depends on the availability of raw materials – basically a particularly vitreous white sand, calcined flint and potash – and the glass houses established themselves on sites where the sand existed naturally in the soil and there were plentiful stands of timber to fire the furnaces and provide the 'pearl ash' or potash made from calcined wood-ash which was a vital ingredient. While Ravenscroft's formula produced a glass described as 'crystal' because of its remarkable brilliance and clarity, it was not as easily workable as Venetian-type 'soda' glass which cooled slowly and could be worked into wonderful shapes. The original intention of English glass-makers had been simply to copy the shapes of Continental glass, but it was soon discovered that the new formula could not be worked in the same way. Thus evolved the plainer shapes of English drinking glasses, from the 'rummer' to early baluster glasses. The 'rummer' was derived from the 'roemer' an early bowl-shaped drinking glass for drinking popular Rhenish wine. The English 'roemer' had a heavy solid stem, unlike the Continental original which was basically a bowl flaring from a cylinder-shaped hollow base, decorated with strawberry prunts and glass thread. The solid-stemmed 'rummer' was soon adapted into a wide variety of bowl-shapes on baluster stems, and made in quantity by all the principal English glass houses, in Bristol, Stafford, Stourbridge, Newcastle, King's Lynn, Henley-on-Thames and London.

Fashion and function

From the capacity of early English drinking glasses such as the rummer, one can guess that wine was drunk 'by the bucket' as well as ale. At the beginning of the 18th century, fortified wines began to come into England from Portugal which required different treatment from clarets and Rhenish wines. Port, sherry and madeira needed decanters with airtight stoppers so that they would keep, and clear glass was required in order to show off their clear, sediment-free colours, as well as smaller glasses to drink them from. Wines were usually served from jugs and ewers filled from the barrel and were often cloudy.

Drinking is convivial, involving toasts, ceremonies and special occasions, and many glasses were engraved with commemorative motifs. English glass was a better medium for engraving than 'soda' glass, and quantities of it were exported, particularly to the Netherlands, for the same purpose. Most wine glasses were made with a conical folded foot during the first three decades of the 18th century. The conical shape lifted the uneven break of the 'pontil' clear of the surface, and the folded foot gave extra strength to the foot rim and was almost impossible to chip.

The 'pontil' was to be found on almost all glasses up to about 1750. It was not part of the finished glass itself, but was added to the blown but still molten piece when the mouth and rim were cut and smoothed, after which the glass was knocked off, leaving a mark where the pontil had been broken off. This slightly jagged mark in the centre of the base had been taken as an infallible guide to dating, but since it is remarkably simple to copy, it should not be taken as definitive proof of age. After about 1750 foot rims were no longer folded but ground flat and the pontil was generally ground off.

The pontil or 'punty' was reintroduced as a genuine part of glass manufacture in the 19th century when press-moulded glass was fire-polished – and incidentally, many reproductions of 18th-century glass were made.

Glass

Periods and styles

It was not fashion which proved the great stimulus to change in English glass, but a swingeing tax of 20 per cent on all clear glass imposed in 1745 which jolted the glassmakers into new methods of making drinking glasses. Before that date the baluster, light or heavy, was the rule, with fluted ale glasses, heavy-footed firing glasses and 'dram' glasses for the increasing consumption of spirits. In addition, 'deceptive' glasses were made for those who felt unequal to drinking a full measure for every toast and still remaining on their feet. There were cordial glasses for strong spirits and tavern 'cans' or mugs for beer and cider, decanters and claret jugs and a great variety of table ware. Decoration was limited to wheel engraving, stipple engraving and diamond engraving, and coloured glass was reserved for the lowly manufacture of wine bottles, dark green or brown. The imprisoned air bubble or teardrop was the only other embellishment, in stems and knops.

After 1745, enamelling took the place of engraving, for a certain amount of glass was wasted in the powder removed by the engraver, and the air bubble was converted into the air-twist stem, a purely English invention which lightened the weight. Coloured glass, exempt from tax, was used for table ware and drinking glasses. Opaque white twists, also tax exempt, were made from *c.*1755, colour twists from about the same period. From about 1760 facet-cut stems were introduced as another method of cutting the weight.

In 1776 the tax on glass was doubled, making it impossible for English glassmakers to continue producing the richer, heavier, cut glass which styles of the day demanded, and in 1780 many of the most famous names in English glassmaking fled to Ireland, which was granted free trade with England. Most of the highly-prized Irish glass, including Waterford, was made by one-time Stourbridge makers, using the same formulae and designs. The quality of the glass differed slightly and was heavier, richer and more brilliant because of the slight increase in lead content. Without the problems of tax to curb their production, Irish glass houses were profligate in cut glass of every kind, rich, heavy and lustrous. The English glass houses with continuing ingenuity resorted to splash enamel, trailed white glass over a coloured body typified by 'Nailsea' glass, and innumerable small novelty pieces made from 'cullet' the waste glass melted down and used again.

Nineteenth-century glass

In 1825 Ireland imposed its own tax on glass, but by this time new techniques had been developed in America and on the Continent, and press-moulding, staining, colouring, flashing and casing were soon used in England to manufacture an entirely new range for the domestic market. Cut glass of heavy quality continued to be in great demand, but around 1830 the cutting became simpler, in plain flutes and horizontal bands, instead of the complex patterns of the beginning of the century. In 1845 the duty on glass was finally removed, and in the few years before the Great Exhibition of 1851 the English glass industry underwent a complete change, introducing a plethora of new techniques, both new and imported, from its new industrial base at Stourbridge.

239

Dates and sequence of baluster shapes

Inverted baluster	1682–1710
Drop knop	1690–1710
Angular knop	1695–1715
Ball knop	1695–1715
Annulated knop (triple ring)	1695–1725
Multiple knops	1700–1720
True baluster	1710–1730
Acorn knop	1710–1715
Silesian stem	1715–1730
Air-twists	from *c.*1745
Opaque white twists	from *c.*1755
Colour twists	from *c.*1755
Facet cut stems	from *c.*1760

Globe-and-shaft shaped
wine bottle in olive green
glass. *c.*1660.
8½ in / 21.5 cm.
£1200–1700.

Green glass plain wine
bottle of mallet shape,
mid- to late 18th century.
£60–80

241

Club-shaped decanter engraved with three-masted man o'war 'Victory' and on the reverse 'Orange Broker', *c.*1810. 12 in / 30.5 cm. £700–1100.

Cut glass decanter with star-cut mushroom stopper, etched with stemmed flowers, from a travelling case *c.*1820. £180–250.

Left A plain ship's decanter with quadruple ring neck and bullseye stopper. 9⁹/₁₆ in / 24 cm. £140–160.

Right Decanter and stopper, the tall neck with single faceted ring, the shoulder cut with printies above flat cutting. 12 in / 30.5 cm. Pair: £130–150.

Cut glass water jug with hobnail panels, fine diamond horizontal slice-cut neck, early 19th century. 8 in / 20.3 cm. £250–350.

Right Victorian English 'rock crystal' jug or ewer with ovoid body engraved with cupids fishing and prunus flower decoration to the faceted neck, c.1870. 10½ in / 27 cm. £300–500.

Claret jug and tapering hexagonal stopper with loop handle, engraved with fruiting vines. 12³⁄₁₆ in / 31 cm. £200–250.

Lemonade jug with plated metal mounts and moulded patterned foot, etched with 'Lemonade' and with ebonised wood handle, designed in the manner of Christopher Dresser. 9¼ in / 23.5 cm. £150–200.

Overlay glass goblet shaped vase in deep red overlaid in white and enamelled in colours, *c.* 1860. 12¾ in/32.5 cm. Bohemian. £500–600.

Goblets

Roemer-shaped goblet engraved with Bacchanalian scene of Silenus lying drunkenly beneath trailing vines, plain stem and cushion knop with tears, on a wide domed foot. Early 18th century. 10⅞ in / 27.5 cm. £800–1000.

Large goblet finely engraved with a portrait of Shakespeare, a full armorial, trailing brambles and a border inscribed 'Not For An Age But For All Time'. 8¹/₁₆ in / 20.5 cm. £100–120.

245

Jacobite portrait firing glass with drawn trumpet bowl and heavy 'firing' foot, *c.*1750. 3¾ in / 9.5 cm. £2500–3500.

Toastmaster's wine glass with deceptive conical bowl and inverted baluster stem with tear in base, on folded conical foot, *c.*1720. 4¾ in / 12 cm. £200–300.

Deceptive glass with funnel bowl, ball knop, short stem with tear, on conical folded foot. *c.*1710–20. 5 in / 12.5 cm. £200–300.

246

Baluster glasses

Baluster wine glass, with bell bowl on a double collar, fine baluster stem with tear, basal knop and folded foot. *c.*1720. 6 in / 15.5 cm. £400–500.

Balustroid cordial glass, the trumpet bowl with solid base containing a tear on a collar and a depressed knop on a plain stem and a basal knop also containing a tear. 6⅝ in / 16.8 cm. £120–150.

Newcastle baluster wine glass, the trumpet bowl with solid base above a beaded knop between two plain knops, a short plain section and a double basal knop, on folded foot. 7⅜ in / 18.8 cm. £350–400.

247

Baluster wine glass with bell bowl, three-ringed annulated knop and basal knop on folded conical foot, *c.*1720. 6 in / 15 cm. £400–500.

Baluster wine glass with round funnel bowl, teared true and inverted baluster knops divided by a collar, on domed and folded foot, *c.*1715. 6 in/15.5 cm. £600–800.

Waisted bucket baluster wine glass with bowl with flattened knop, collar, and teared dumbell knop on folded spreading foot, *c.*1720. 5¼ in / 13.5 cm. £400–600.

Air-twist glasses

Wine glass with drawn trumpet bowl engraved with a wide border of fruiting vine, on multiple air twist stem. 7$\frac{1}{16}$ in/18 cm. £200–250.

Tall toasting glass with slim drawn trumpet bowl and multiple spiral air-twist stem. *c.*1750. 7$\frac{1}{2}$ in/19 cm. £300–400.

Wine glass with round funnel bowl and loose spiral gauze opaque twist. 6 in/15 cm. £100–140.

Above Wine glass with slender bell bowl, shoulder and centre knop and multiple spiral air-twist stem on conical folded foot, *c.*1750. 6½ in/16.5 cm. £200–300.

Above, right Wine glass with round funnel bowl, shoulder knop and multiple spiral air-twist stem on conical foot, *c.*1750. 6⅛ in/15.7 cm. £150–200.

Wine glass with flared bucket bowl diamond-point engraved with simple leaf sprays, on an opaque twist stem with a central air thread. 6½ in/16.5 cm. £140–160.

Wine glass with ogee bowl, on an opaque twist stem composed of a gauze corkscrew within two solid tapes. 6⁵/₁₆ in/16 cm. £100–130.

Cordial glass, the rounded funnel with basal flutes, on an opaque twist stem composed of a gauze corkscrew encircled by solid spiral tapes. 6¹¹/₁₆ in/17 cm. £150–200.

Electioneering glass with ogee bowl engraved with fruiting vine and 'Shafto & Vane Forever' with double series opaque twist stem on conical foot. 6⅛ in/15.7 cm. £700–1000.

Rare colour twist wine glass with round funnel bowl, the stem with central six-ply canary yellow twist within a pair of six-ply opaque white corkscrews, on conical foot, *c.*1750–60. 6 in/15 cm. £1800–2200.

Colour twist wine glass with small rounded funnel bowl, the stem composed of a central red ribbon within a pair of six-ply corkscrews. 5⅞ in/15 cm. £600–800.

Wine glass with round funnel bowl with opaque white corkscrew twist with deep red and white spiral bands, on conical folded foot. 6⅛ in/15.7 cm. £500–600.

'Jacobite' glasses

Jacobite wine glass
with drawn trumpet
bowl engraved with
six-petalled rose, one
bud and a leaf, on
plain stem with tear,
on folded conical
foot, *c.*1740–50.
5½in/14cm.
£400–600.

Wine glass with
diamond-faceted
stem and round
funnel bowl engraved
with six-petalled rose
and leaves and two
buds, on plain conical
foot, *c.*1770.
6in/15cm.
£200–300.

'Jacobite' glasses

Jacobite glass, wheel-engraved with a rose, a half rose, a bud and an oak leaf inscribed 'Fiat' with an air-twist stem on conical foot, c. 1745. 5⅝ in/14.5 cm. £500–800.

Wine glass engraved with six-petalled rose and bud and bird in flight with opaque twist stem on conical foot, c. 1755. 5½ in/14 cm. £400–600.

Ale glasses and coloured wine glass

Wine glass with drawn trumpet bowl, green-tinted glass with multiple spiral air-twist stem on conical foot, *c.*1760. 7 in / 18 cm. £600–800.

Ale glass with round funnel bowl and colour twist stem with threads of opaque white, blue and deep canary yellow, *c.*1760–70. 7⅞ in/20 cm. £1500–2000.

Ale glass with tall round funnel bowl engraved with hops and barley, with opaque twist stem, *c.*1760. 6⅝ in / 17 cm. £200–250.

Cordial and ale glasses

Cordial glass, the small ogee bowl engraved with a spray of blackcurrants, probably signifying the cordial, on an opaque twist stem of a gauze cable encircled by a multi-ply spiral strand. 5½ in/14 cm. £150–200.

Ale glass with tall ogee bowl with basal fluting, on double series opaque twist stem, *c.*1760. 7⅛ in/18.3 cm. £200–250.

Cordial glass with drawn trumpet bowl and mercurial air-twist stem, *c.*1740–50. 6⅝ in/17 cm. £200–300.

Decorative engraved glass

Wine glass with lipped round funnel bowl with basal cutting and hexagonal faceted stem, with lobed faceted foot, *c.*1775–80. 6 in / 15.5 cm. £150–180.

Wine glass with pan-topped bowl engraved with floral meander on multiple spiral airtwist stem with swelled knop, on plain conical foot, *c.*1760. 5½ in / 14 cm. £300–400.

An 18th-century German engraved glass tankard with pewter foot-rim and border, with pewter lid, dated 1763. £400–600.

Bohemian clear glass tankard in the manner of and possibly by Franz Zach, the cylindrical body deeply cut and engraved with a stag and two does in a woodland clearing surrounded by hills, stout loop handle and flat plain glass cover, pewer mount. 6½ in/16.5 cm. £1000–2000.

Paperweights

a Clichy small concentric paperweight with a central pale blue cane surrounded by two rows of brightly coloured canes including a 'Clichy rose', on a latticinio muslin ground. 2⅜ in/6 cm. £200–300.

b Baccarat pansy paperweight, the flower with two dark purple petals and three yellow petals with purple spots, a single yellow and purple bud and bright green leaves, star cut base. 2½ in/6.5 cm. £250–350.

a

b

c

d

e

f

c Baccarat garland weight with a central green cane within a circle of blue canes, surrounded by six circles of white canes enclosing alternate red and white canes. 2¾ in/7 cm. £200–300.

e Clichy close millefiori paperweight with the multi-coloured canes set in a basket of dark blue and white staves. 2½ in/6.5 cm. £400–600.

d Clichy swirl paperweight with blue and white staves radiating from a central pink and white cane. 2¾ in/7 cm. £250–350.

f Baccarat primrose paperweight, the flower with six dark blue petals with white crescents, surrounded by six green leaves, on a stem with six leaves, star cut base. 2½ in/6.5 cm. £300–400.

Cameo glass

Stourbridge cameo glass vase in light olive green overlaid thinly in white, c.1880. 5 in/12.5 cm. £600–800.

Below Cameo scent bottle, Stourbridge, with 'cracked ice' body overlaid in white and deep red, with silver mounts, c.1890. £800–1000.

Stourbridge cameo glass oil lamp in white glass cased in deep raspberry red and overlaid with white, on three clear glass feet, c.1880–90. £600–800.

Thomas Webb cameo vase with yellow ground overlaid in
white. Moulded mark, *c.*1880. 3½in/8.9cm. £700–1000.

Thomas Webb 'four layer' cameo glass with white base cased
in yellow, red and white, *c.*1880. 6in/15.5cm. £800–1000.

Left to right Stourbridge peachblow satin glass vase. £200–250. Stevens and Williams swirl satin bowl, £150–180, and vase, £200–250. All *c.*1880.

Citreen-ground cameo glass scent bottle of slender tapering form, the white overlay carved with a leafy stem with harebell-like flowers on one side, the reverse with a leafy stem, silver neck mount and hinged cover. Silver London 1884, maker's mark John Newton Mappin. 5⅞in/15cm. £300–320.

Cameo glass scent bottle of slender tapering form, in blue glass overlaid in white and carved with a spray of flowers and leaves on one side, the reverse with a stem of long thin leaves, American silver mount and screw-on cover engraved with a monogram, by Gorham of Massachusetts. 6⁵⁄₁₆in/ 16cm. £280–300.

Above A pair of claret jugs in 'Rock Crystal' style, *c.*1870.
£700–1000 single. *Below* 'Rock Crystal' style ewer, *c.*1870.
£1800–2400.

Triple-overlay cameo glass
vase with formalized flowers
and leaves overlaid on matt
ground £600–800.

Glass vase of ovoid shape
overlaid in pink and brown
with brambles on a smokey
pink ground, signed Gallé.
£1500–2000.

Gallé cameo landscape vase
overlaid in brown on a
smokey matt background, th
tall neck flaring towards the
mouth. £1200–1500.

Fine large Lalique glass vase with metal mount, of 'Aigrettes' pattern. 9½ in/24 cm. £750–1000.

Frosted glass figure 'Source de la Fontaine'. £1500–2000.

Glossary

Acanthus Leaf pattern derived from Greek and Roman design.

Act of Parliament clock Large wall-clock with wooden face and short case, named after tax briefly imposed on clocks and watches in 1797.

Acid engraving, acid etching In glass, where acid is used to produce similar results to true engraving, but with thin shallow lines. In silver, a similar process.

Adam style Neo-classical style attributed largely to the Adam brothers from *c.*1750s.

Air-twist Glasses with stems drawn from air bubbles into spiralling threads.

Alloy A combination of two or more metals.

Ale glass Tall slender glass for drinking strong ale, not beer.

Amorini Little baroque figures of angelic boys, as distinct from cupids or cherubs.

Anchor escapement See Escapement.

Animalier Resembling an animal, as spouts of tea and coffee pots.

Anneal The process of heating and quenching metal to keep it malleable while being worked.

Anthemion Stylised honeysuckle motif from classical Greek ornament.

Apostle spoon Popular finial from medieval times onwards for spoons.

Applied, applied relief Ornament, decoration, made separately and added.

Apron Shaped ornamental piece between front legs of stand, chair, table, etc.

Arabesque Elaborately intertwined stylised foliage and flowers.

Arcade Arch-shaped decoration.

Ark A slope-lidded chest, originally made by an arkwright.

Armoire Continental term for clothes press or cupboard.

Armorial Coat of arms, crests, heraldic badges.

Assay, Assay Office Test or trial of metals for purity – the Assay Office carried out the tests.

Astragal Small half-round moulding or beading – also most common type of glazing bars for glass cabinet doors.

Aumbry Food storage cupboard with bars to doors for ventilation.

Automata Mechanically-operated clockwork devices.

Bachelor's chest Small chest of drawers with folding top opening out as writing surface.

Backplate Metal plate behind handles and drawer pulls. In

clocks the back plate of a movement, often beautifully engraved.

Bail handle Simple half-round swing handle or drawer pull.

Ball-and-claw Originally dragon's claw grasping pearl, adapted with eagle's claw and lion's paw for feet of cabriole legs.

Balloon back Waisted chairback.

Bamboo See Caneware.

Baluster Pillar with vase or pear-shaped swelling, as chair and table legs of late 17th and 18th century and as stems of drinking glasses from *c.*1680, also as shape of silver hollow ware.

Banding See Cross-banding.

Baroque Florid style originating on the Continent, evident in English design from *c.*1660–1730 and some silver of same period.

Basal knop Knop at base of stem.

Basalte Fine black stoneware developed from 'Egyptian black' by Josiah Wedgwood *c.*1760. Revived in 19th century as 'basalt'.

Bat Printing Development of over-glaze transfer-printing using a 'bat' or flexible sheet composed of glue, whiting and treacle.

Bayonet fitting Secure method of fixing pierced tops of dredgers to bases, as light bulbs fix into sockets.

Beading Continuous row of half-rounds like a bead necklace.

Bellarmine Originating in Germany, brownish salt-glazed stoneware flasks or bottles with relief mask, copied in England from 17th–19th century.

Bergere Low-backed chair with back and arms in continuous curve.

Bifurcated Forked.

Biggin Squat-shaped coffee pot with short pouring lip from *c.*1796, originally on stands with lamps.

Billet Thumbpiece on tankard or flagon.

Bilston enamel From *c.*1740 enamel made in the Birmingham/Bilston area.

Birdcage In clocks, the upright pillar construction holding the movement between two plates. In tables, a similar construction with hinge to allow table top to tilt, lift off or revolve.

Biscuit, bisque Once-fired unglazed porcelain ware.

Bleeding bowl Small shallow bowl with single handle or 'ear'.

Block front Cabinet doors with solid wooden panels and no glazing. Originally referred to solid wooden fronts on different planes, as breakfront.

Blown moulded In glass, vessels shaped by blowing glass into a metal mould. Used from 17th century onwards with one-piece moulds and from *c.*1800 with two-piece moulds when the inner surface was completely smooth and did not follow the contours of outside configurations.

Blue dash charger Dutch pattern Delftware with rims of plates, bowls, sponged with diagonal lines of blue suggesting ropework. Much copied in England in 17th and 18th century.

Bobbin turning, reel turning Turned uprights with continuous swell and ring shape like rounded cotton reels.

Body Any basic clay mix for earthenware and stoneware. In porcelain and bone china, called 'paste'.

Bolt and shutter Device to keep clock movement going when the shutter covering the winding hole is opened.

Glossary

Bombé French term for chests with swelling outline both vertically and horizontally.

Bone china From *c.*1794 the paste used for English tableware.

Bonheur du jour Light ladies' writing cabinet on four tall slender legs.

Boulle, Buhl Tortoiseshell and brass or silver marquetry made originally by André Charles Boulle (1642–1732). 'Premiere partie' is tortoiseshell inlaid with metal, 'contre partie' is metal inlaid with tortoiseshell.

Bow front Furniture with convex curve horizontally.

Bracket clock Spring-driven clocks without long pendulums made to stand on a table or shelf.

Bracket foot Shaped like a wooden shelf bracket, used on chests and cabinets, etc.

Braganza scroll Rather ornate, compressed S-scroll.

Bramah lock Barrel lock used on English furniture from *c.*1784.

Break front Furniture with the central section stepped slightly forward.

Bright cut Technique of engraving with minutely faceted cutting, much used in silver in latter part of 18th century.

Britannia standard Higher ratio of pure silver metal in silver plate enforced from 1697–1720, marked with a figure of Britannia seated.

British plate Variation of Sheffield plate using nickel alloy instead of copper as the core, patented in 1836.

Broken pediment Pediment broken in centre sometimes with pedestal for urn, bust or decorative feature.

Brushing slide Pull-out surface just below top of chest of drawers and above top drawer.

Bull's eye In clocks, the small glass aperture through which the pendulum can be seen in a longcase clock. In glass, the thickened centre of a sheet of Crown glass.

Bull's eye stopper Distinctive shape of decanter stopper, disc-shaped with wavy edge, thinning to a hole in centre.

Bun foot Ball-shaped foot to furniture, common in late 17th century and revived by Victorians.

Burmese glass Opaque heat-shaded glass toning from pale yellow to deep pink, made by Thomas Webb & Sons under US patent.

Burnished Gold, silver or gilding polished with hardstone to give a brilliant finish.

Burr Veneer cut from the root with distinctive figure and patterning.

Cabaret set In bone china, more rarely porcelain, teaset for one or two people, including a matching tray.

Cabinet ware Decorative ceramics of high artistic standard for display only, not for use.

Cabriole leg Shape of furniture leg based on cyma curve, using spring of solid wood cut away to curve outwards at knee, tapering slightly and curving inwards above the foot.

Calyx Cup-like shape of leaves enclosing bud or flower.

Cameo glass Two-colour glass with white over dark base, the white, cut or acid-etched to varying degrees of thickness.

Campagna Bell-shaped Greek vase, a shape popular in neo-classical designs of Regency period.

Candle slide Small pull-out tray to hold candlestick.

Cane In glass, coloured or opaque rods used in making

Glossary

colour-twist glasses and paperweights.

Caneware In ceramics, straw-coloured dry stoneware developed by Josiah Wedgwood, used for making tableware and bamboo-ware.

Canted corner A corner cut off diagonally, on a slanting plane, on chests, cabinets, etc.

Capstan Cylindrical shape curving inwards at the waist.

Carcase Basic structure of a piece of furniture, often in cheaper wood, then veneered.

Carlton House desk Writing table with D-shaped superstructure, on tapering legs, of late 18th-century design.

Carolean Applied to designs of Charles I and Charles II periods.

Cartel clock Ornate French wall clock adapted in England with giltwood frames instead of ormolu.

Cartouche Framework or surround to coat of arms or crest. The term also used to describe similar-shaped frame enclosing decorative motif.

Cased glass Glass overlaid with one or more colours, one of which was usually white, and cut away to show colour beneath. Also called 'flashed' glass.

Cast Solid metal made in a mould, as distinct from sheet metal.

Caster Container with perforated top for sprinkling sugar, pepper, etc.

Castor Small wheel set in brass socket or between brass arms on base of furniture.

Cellarette Compartmented container to hold wine bottles, from Georgian period onwards.

Chamber stick Candle holder on low stem set in wide dish, often with slot for snuffers or extinguisher cap.

Chamfered Similar to 'canted' but of legs of tables, chairs, etc.

Charger Large deep-bowled serving dish.

Chased, chasing Decoration in high or low relief using blunt tools to shape metal, often used in conjunction with embossing. No metal is removed in process, unlike engraving. Flat-chasing is the decorating of a surface using this technique instead of engraving.

Cheveret Narrow writing tables with drawers and pigeon holes similar but more sturdy to bonheur du jour.

Chiffonier Low side cabinet with shelves or doors below a marble top.

Chiming clock A clock chiming quarters as well as hours.

China stone Ingredient of hard-paste porcelain.

Chinese lattice Geometric asymmetrical lattice, sometimes called 'cracked ice'.

Chinoiserie Recurring fashion for European versions of Oriental designs.

Chip carving Shallow, geometric carving on early English oak furniture.

Cobalt Blue pigment used for ceramic decoration and 'Bristol blue' coloured glass.

Cockbead Small usually half-round mouldings, generally round drawer-fronts from c.1730.

Cockshead hinge S-shaped hinge, originally in iron, later in brass.

Coffee can Straight-sided mug-shaped cup.

Coffered panel A panel which is sunk in its frame, opposite of 'fielded'.

270

Collar Small moulding around vertical part of piece of furniture, usually table legs. Also called 'gaitered'.

Commode From the French, an elegant chest on short legs made in England from *c.*1740.

Contre partie See Boulle.

Console Table fixed to the wall and supported on decorative front bracket legs.

Cordial glass Small-bowled drinking glass for strong aromatic drinks similar to liqueurs.

Cornice Decorative or plain moulding below the pediment.

Cottages Pastille burners, money boxes, souvenirs, made in bone china or Staffordshire pottery.

Count wheel A wheel in the striking mechanism of a clock.

Court cupboard From the 16th century an open cupboard for displaying plate, often wrongly called a 'buffet'.

Cow's horn stretcher See Crinoline stretcher.

Crabstock Handles of tea and coffee pots shaped like a gnarled crab-apple branch.

Cracked ice See Chinese lattice.

Creamware Developed by Josiah Wedgwood from *c.*1760 from yellow-buff clays with cream-coloured glaze *c.*1764 making it non-porous and hardwearing.

Credence table Small flap side table opening to a circular or hexagonal top.

Credenza From late medieval period, a cupboard for storing food, hence an Italian side-cupboard, often ornately decorated.

Crest rail Top horizontal rail of a chairback.

Crinoline stretcher Half-hoop stretcher common on Windsor chairs.

Cross-banding Strips of veneer edging table tops, drawer fronts, etc. cut across the grain to prevent lifting and shrinking.

Cullet Broken glass melted down for cost-cutting reasons in glass-making.

Cushion drawer Drawer with no pulls in cornice of escritoires, late 17th and early 18th century.

Cut card work Decoration on silver using thin sheets of silver cut into shapes of foliage, scrolls, etc. and applied (soldered) on to vessels to produce relief ornament without casting from *c.*1660 onwards.

Cutlery Any eating implement with a cutting edge.

Cyma curve Also known as ogee, ogive, an S-shaped curve, concave above, convex below.

Cymric silver Made for Liberty & Co mainly with mechanical processes for decorative 'Art Nouveau' objects.

Davenport Small, low, compact ladies' desk made from *c.*1789.

Deceptive glass Small glass with thickened bowl for making small drinks look larger, i.e. for Toastmasters.

Delftware English earthenware associated with Delft, Holland.

Demilune Half circular.

Dentil Cornice moulding with repeating raised rectangular blocks like teeth.

Dial plate The whole part of a clock face on which the chapter ring and spandrels are fixed.

Diamond-point engraving Engraving with a fine diamond-pointed tool on glass to achieve a stippled effect.

Diaper Repeated lozenge, diamond or trellis design.

Glossary

Dish ring Hollow, waisted cylinder in silver and other metals to hold warm plates and dishes clear of polished surfaces. As 'potato ring' it was placed on a dish lined with a napkin and filled with jacket potatoes.

Dished Concave shaping, on solid wooden chair seats, candle slides, on games tables to hold counters.

Distressed Trade term for damaged piece of furniture or surface.

Douter Cone-shaped candle extinguisher.

Dowel Wooden peg used to secure frame of furniture.

Dram glass Small glass with heavy foot and short thick stem holding 2oz spirits.

Drawn stem, bowl In glasses where the stem and bowl are made in one part and not separately when it is known as 'stuck shank'.

Draw-leaf table, draw table Table extending with two leaves which pull out from beneath central section.

Dredger Correctly, a kitchen caster with a loop handle, but term also used for sugar casters, etc.

Drop-in seat Seat of chair made with separate wooden frame.

Dumb waiter Two or three small circular tiers on a central tripod pillar.

Dummy drawer A mock drawer, usually to match up one on the opposite side, so appearing to be a pair.

Earthenware Clay wares which are porous after firing and therefore need glazing.

Ebonised Painted or stained to resemble ebony.

Electroplate Base metal coated with a thin layer of pure silver by electro-chemical galvanic action, from *c.*1840.

Electrotype Costly process using similar process to electro-plating to reproduce rare original casts – also known as electro-forming, patented 1841.

Embossing Technique of raising relief decoration by hammering and punching sheet metal on a bed of pitch, usually finished more crisply on the outer surface, a process known as repoussé.

Enamel Clear glass, coloured or made opaque with pigments which subsequently fuses to the surface of glass, ceramics or metal.

Encaustic Decoration achieved by burning-in pigments to earthenware.

Engine-turned Close line patterns incised on fine stoneware or silver using a lathe.

Entrée dish Serving dish in silver, Cheffield plate, ceramics, with close-fitting lid.

Épergne Table centrepiece, frequently ornate, consisting of tiers of dishes on a central frame from which hang small baskets and dishes, from *c.*1760 onwards.

EPNS Electro-plated nickel silver.

Escapement The mechanism of a clock which allows the train to move at regular intervals. Anchor escapement from *c.*1670 allowed a long pendulum to swing in a narrow arc. Verge escapement has a crown wheel with teeth which allow the escape to pass at regular intervals, used with short bob pendulums.

Escutcheon Keyhole plate – also a shield shape for armorials.

Ewer Tall jug on pedestal foot.

Glossary

Facet, facet cutting Shallow hollows ground or cut in stems, etc. of glasses to make diamond pattern.

Façon de Venise Intricate vessels and objects made in fragile soda glass in Murano from 13th century onwards, imitated in England in 19th century.

Fall front A desk or bureau with a downward-hinging writing surface.

False pendulum Small disc attached to pendulum where it passes aperture in dial, set above pendulum itself.

Famille rose, famille vert Chinese porcelain in colours dominated by soft pink or green, the term adopted by English potteries from *c.*1720.

Fan cut Glass cut in fan shapes.

Felspar porcelain From *c.*1800 developed by Spode to modify bone china with pure felspar to produce brilliantly white, extremely hard wares.

Festoon An altogether lighter version of a swag.

Fiddle pattern Back splat of chair, terminal of silver flatware shaped like a violin.

Fielded panel Panel with bevelled or chamfered edges, the centre standing out in the frame.

Filled Another term for loaded.

Finial Top ornament, i.e. urn, flambeau, etc. on top of furniture, lids of silver and porcelain, clocks, etc.

Fire polishing Reheated moulded glass polished to remove mould marks thereby suggesting hand-cut or blown work.

Firing glass Glass used for toasts accompanied by rapping on the table like gunfire – thick and stumpy with heavy stem and disc foot, from *c.*1760 onwards.

Flatware In silverware, all tableware without a cutting edge. In porcelain, plates and flat dishes as distinct from hollow ware.

Flambeau Spiralling flame shape.

Flashing See Casing.

Flint glass Developed by George Ravenscroft *c.*1685, a pure brilliant glass containing lead oxide, also called lead crystal.

Flute glass Drinking glass with deep conical bowl on slender stem, for drinking cider or strong ale.

Fluted, fluting Close-set grooves, as on classical pillars.

Fly bracket Small brackets supporting narrow leaves of tables.

Folded foot Glass with domed or conical foot with outside rim turned under.

Foliate Pattern or design with leaves.

Fret, fretted Openwork pattern, usually geometrical.

Frieze, frieze drawer In furniture, the horizontal part below a cabinet cornice or below a table top. The frieze drawer is set below the table top in the frieze.

Fruitwood Wood from orchard trees such as apple and pear.

Fusee In clocks, the cone-shaped piece of metal with a spiral track, round which the gut or chain winds as it comes off the spring barrel.

Gadroon Repetitive lobes either upright or slanting, suggesting the knuckles of a clenched fist.

Gaitered See Collar.

Gallery Raised border or miniature balustrade in wood or metal.

Garniture Set of three or more decorative urns, vases, for a mantel or cabinet.

Glossary

Gate leg The hinged legs and stretchers which pivot out from the main frame of a table to support the hinged flaps or leaves.

Gilt metal Base metal which has been gilded, not necessarily ormolu.

Glaze Coating of glass-like transparency making earthenware non-porous and fusing to the body or paste of porcelain to fix the decoration beneath.

Glazing bars The bars holding panes of glass into a door of a cabinet.

Gothic A style associated with medieval German design, of pointed arches and pinnacles.

Grande sonnerie A clock chiming or striking both hour and quarter hour every quarter.

Great wheel In clock movements, the first wheel of the going train.

Greek key, Greek fret Rigidly stylised wave pattern composed of straight lines.

Green glaze ware Developed by Josiah Wedgwood for table ware particularly in leaf shapes from *c.*1764.

Grille Lattice of brass wire.

Guilloche Repeating ornament of intertwined ribbons making a series of small circles.

Hall chair, seat With solid wooden seat and back, often painted with armorials.

Hallmark Assay Office mark signifying that silver has come up to standard of purity.

Harlequin set A set of tableware with each piece in the same design but a different colour or pattern.

Harlequin table Version of the Pembroke table with small rising section containing pigeonholes and drawers.

Hard-paste porcelain 'True' porcelain first made in England at Plymouth *c.*1768 but difficult to work and soon superseded by bone china.

Heavy baluster First series of baluster-stemmed wine glasses made from *c.*1680.

Hobnail cutting Pattern of cut glass with deep incisions, cross-cut to form eight-pointed stars.

Hollow ware In all table ware, hollow vessels as opposed to flatware.

Hood In clocks, the upper removable part of a longcase clock enclosing the dial.

Huguenot French Protestants fleeing from the Revocation of the Edict of Nantes in 1685, including many fine craftsmen and silversmiths escaping to England from religious persecution.

Imari pattern 18th-century Japanese export porcelain much copied in English 'Japan pattern' by Worcester, Derby, etc.

'Improve' Later Victorian decoration to mainly 18th-century silver and furniture.

Incised ornament Cut, carved or engraved as opposed to 'applied'.

Inlay Decorative patterns cut in surface of solid wood and inset with contrasting woods, metals, ivory, etc.

'In the white' Once-fired porcelain often decorated by artists outside the pottery or factory.

Ironstone china Patented by C. J. Mason in 1813, strong white hard-wearing earthenware, slightly transparent and heavy.

Glossary

Jacobite Engraving, painting, supporting the cause of the Old and Young Pretenders, particularly the 1745 Rebellion.

Japanning A finish composed of layers of varnish on coloured grounds decorated with 'chinoiserie' on English furniture, clock cases.

Japan pattern See Imari, Kakiemon.

Jasper ware Dense fine stoneware needing no glaze introduced by Josiah Wedgwood *c.*1774, tinted throughout the body in pale blue, green, lilac. Later imitations were 'jasper dip' with colour on surface from dipping in jasper slip.

Kakiemon Design of Chinese origin adapted by Japanese potters, patterns widely copied by English potters.

Knee In chairs, tables, etc. the top of the leg which curves outwards.

Knop In glass, decorative shapes on stems – acorn, mushroom, cushion, etc. In silver, decorative finial cast and soldered to straight handles of early spoons.

Kylin Japanese dragon device used in pottery and porcelain patterns and as decorative handles.

Lacquer Should only describe Japanese work, but in general covers English Japanning as well.

Lambeth Delft General name for London-made Delftware.

Lancet clock Regency bracket clock shape with Gothic pointed arched case.

Lantern clock Early weight-driven clock made from *c.*1630–*c.*1730 with posted 'birdcage' frame and brass case topped by a single bell.

Late-embossed In silver, earlier wares which have been embossed at a later date, usually Victorian.

Latticino In glass, ancient technique of enclosing fine threads of opaque or coloured glass in clear glass – used to describe Nailsea glass with trailed white decoration.

Lead glass See Flint glass.

Lenticle Proper term for 'bull's eye' aperture in the waist door of a longcase clock.

Light baluster Taller, slimmer version of heavy baluster glass typified by 'Newcastle' glasses.

Linenfold Formal representations of folds of cloth on carved panels from late 15th century, revived 19th century.

Lion's mask Decorative motif used in silver and on furniture mounts, particularly drawer pulls.

Lip moulding Similar to thumb moulding.

Loaded Sheet metal filled with pitch, e.g. silver and Sheffield plate candlesticks.

Lopers Supports to fall-fronts, brushing slides, etc.

Low relief Carved or embossed decoration projecting only slightly from the surface.

Lunar dial On clocks, the dial showing phases of the moon.

Lunette Half-moon shaped decoration.

Lustre ware Generally describes pottery from Staffordshire and Sunderland decorated with metallic salts and fired to give gold, silver or copper-like finish.

Lyre end, lyre back Shaped like a musical lyre.

Maintaining power In clocks, a device to keep the movement going while being wound. See Bolt and shutter.

Glossary

Majolica, Maiolica Early Italian tin-glazed earthenware similar to Delft. The anglicised 'majolica' generally applies to brightly-coloured relief-moulded wares developed by Minton *c.*1851.

Marquetry Decorative patterns inset into a single sheet of veneer cut to receive the different coloured pieces.

'Marriage' Trade term for piece of furniture made up from parts of similar pieces, i.e. bureau, bookcase, etc.

Marrow scoop Long narrow scoop in heavy-gauge silver for scooping marrow from bones, sometimes combined with a spoon.

Martinware Salt-glazed stoneware 'grotesques' and other ware made by the Martin Brothers at Southall *c.*1877–1915.

Mask Decorative motif derived from classical masks worn in Greek theatre.

Master glass Sweetmeat glass at the top of a table centrepiece, sometimes called Orange glass.

Matt, matting In silver and on clock faces, small punch-marks covering surface giving textured finish.

Mazarine In silver and ceramics a strainer dish pierced in decorative patterns, placed beneath a fish to drain juices, less frequently beneath fowl or joint.

Mazarine blue Rich dark blue, applied to soft-paste porcelain biscuit.

Mean time Time recorded by mechanical methods giving hours of equal length.

Meissen German porcelain factory near Dresden which first made hard-paste porcelain successfully in Europe *c.*1710.

Mercury twist Air-twist stems incorporating canes of exceptionally brilliant glass resembling mercury.

Milled In silver, finished like the rims of coins.

Millefiore Ornamental glass, usually paperweights, made using canes of many-coloured glass.

Mons In porcelain, centre of a dish, plate or bowl, usually slightly raised.

Monteith Large silver bowl with detachable notched or scalloped rim for holding wine glasses by their stems with their their bowls in iced water.

Mortise and tenon In furniture, joining end-grain to side grain with a tongue slotting into second piece, usually at right angles, secured by pegs or dowels.

Mote spoon Long-handled spoon with pierced bowl and pointed end for skimming poured tea and unblocking spout strainer of teapot.

Moulded In glass and ceramics, blown, pressed or cast in a mould. In furniture, decoratively shaped sections of applied ornament are known as 'mouldings'.

Mount Term usually used to describe metals used in association with other materials in a decorative form.

Murano Venetian glass-making centre from 13th century.

Nailsea glass Fancy glass including rolling pins, walking sticks, gemmel flasks in imitation 'latticino' – inaccurate descriptive term.

Nankin blue Name for ancient capital of China from which great quantities of blue-and-white wares were exported to England.

Nottingham ware Heavy, functional, brown stoneware.

Octafoil Eight lobed, as in 'trefoil'.

Ogee, Ogive See cyma curve.

Opal, opaline Semi-opaque glass with fiery glow like gemstone.

Ormolu Bronze fire-gilded with powdered gold in elaborately decorative furniture mounts, clock cases, etc. English equivalent is usually gilt brass or gilt metal.

Overlay Glass cased or 'flashed' in different colours.

Ovolo Convex moulding of quarter-round section.

Oyster veneer Veneer cut from small branches with fine figuring and grain, resembling oyster shells.

Pad foot Simple rounded out-turned foot to furniture.

Palladian Style of architecture based on classical Roman by Andrea Palladio in 16th century greatly influencing early Georgian and Adam design.

Parcel gilt Partially gilded, usually of silver.

Parian ware Vitrified porcelain simulating white Grecian marble from Paros made from *c.*1842 for portrait busts, shaped in moulds.

Parquetry Veneers cut in geometrical patterns, as in 'parquet floor'.

Paste Substance forming the 'body' of porcelain.

Pastille burner Small model, usually of cottage or summer house in bone china or pottery, in which aromatic pastilles were burned.

Patera Small circular ornament, flat or in low relief.

Pâte-sur-pâte Similar technique in ceramics to cameo glass, with white semi-transparent slip over a coloured ground, pared or cut away to show tones of body colour.

Patina Build-up of centuries' gloss and polish from use and wear.

Paw foot Shaped like a lion's paw.

Pearlware Tough white earthenware with faint translucence called by J. Wedgwood 'an improvement on creamware' and ideal for transfer-printing.

Pedestal foot, base Solid base to furniture without feet, but shaped like the base of a pedestal.

Pediment The topmost part of cabinet furniture above the cornice.

Pegged Fixed, as in mortise and tenon joints, with pegs or dowels.

Petite sonnerie Striking on two bells of different tones to denote each quarter, also known as 'ting tang strike'.

Petuntse Ingredient of hard-paste porcelain.

Piecrust In furniture, silver, rims carved in a series of cyma curves.

Piecrust ware Made by Wedgwood *c.*1770 to resemble standing pies, copied by other potteries from 1830s onwards.

Pierced Openwork decoration in silver, wood, etc.

Pillar In clocks, the upright posts supporting the front and back plates of the movement.

Pillar-and-claw Originally described small tripod stands for tables, etc., now also for pillar supports for dining tables.

Pitch Resinous tarry substance used for 'filling' or 'loading' candlesticks, and as working base on which silversmiths could chase and emboss.

Planishing Smoothing, polishing surface of finished silver by hammering with slightly convex planishing hammer.

Glossary

Plated Of silver, generally implies electro-plated.

'Plate' The name by which all articles in silver and gold are known.

Plates In clocks, the two flat metal pieces which contain the movement.

Plinth Square or rectangular base to furniture.

Polychrome Many colours.

Pontil Dab of molten glass used to fix glass vessels to a rod during finishing. Pontil mark is the uneven break mark where the pontil has been snapped off.

Porcelain White paste as opposed to earthenware body.

Porringer Two-handled cup with or without lid and saucer, in silver, pottery and porcelain in all shapes and sizes, for semi-solid gruels, etc. A 'caudle cup' is strictly speaking for liquids.

Posted movement, frame In clocks, where the plates are horizontal and held by four or more corner pillars or posts.

Prattware Made by many potters from *c.*1790–1830s, brightly-coloured pottery, jugs, figures, etc., now generally attribute to Felix Pratt.

Premiere partie See Boulle.

Press A large cupboard for linen, clothes, etc.

Press moulded Thick, heavy glass in imitation of cut glass introduced from *c.*1830, finished by fire-polishing with legitimate use of pontil, not intended to suggest old glass.

Provenance History of an antique and proof of previous ownership.

Provincial clock Made anywhere outside London.

Prunt Small applied decoration to early drinking glasses, often called 'strawberry prunt' because of their shape.

Pseudo oriental, Chinese Mock character marks on Oriental style porcelain.

Pull repeat, push repeat Clocks with striking mechanisms activated at any time by pulling a cord or pushing a button.

Punched, punched work Decoration round rim of silver punched from the back to raise rows of hollow beading.

Putti Small cherubs, cupids, on Baroque and Renaissance designs.

Quarter veneer Veneer laid in four quarters instead of a single piece.

Quartetto tables Four small tables in graduated sizes fitting into each other.

'Queen Anne' Style covering period 1700–20 and revived in 19th century, now generally called 'Queen Anne Style'.

Rack strike Mechanism of a clock striking train activated by a serrated wheel, introduced 1676.

Rail In furniture, horizontal parts of a frame – e.g. crest rail of a chair.

Raising In silversmithing, the making of hollow ware by hammering and shaping on a 'raising stake'.

Ratafia glass Tall flute glass of small capacity for almond-flavoured cordial.

Reeding Parallel close-set convex moulding, the opposite of fluting.

Regulator (clock) Weight-driven pendulum clock with no striking mechanism with dead-beat escapement and compensating pendulum for extremely accurate timekeeping.

Repoussé See Chasing, Embossing.

278

Glossary

Reserve, reserving In ceramics, the part of the decoration not covered by the ground colour.

Ring-turned Rings round columns, stems, legs, made on a lathe.

Rise and fall dial Small dial on clock face for raising and lowering pendulum thus regulating speed of movement.

Rising top Term originally used by 18th-century and 19th-century cabinet-makers for part of furniture which rose by mechanical means, now generally for any part of superstructure additional to basic design.

Roemer German glass with wide hollow stem for drinking Rhenish wines, usually pale green in colour.

Rope twist Decorative device to commemorate Nelson's victories from *c.*1805.

Rummer Deep-bowled English glass on short stem with wide foot for drinking rum punches.

Sabre leg Chair leg with concave curve in the shape of a scimitar or sabre.

Salt-glaze Non-porous glaze achieved by throwing salt into pottery kiln at maximum temperature so that it vitrifies.

Salver A small tray on a single central foot.

Scale, salmon scale Small design resembling fish scales used extensively in Worcester porcelain patterns to break up areas of dark blue grounds, less frequently pink, from *c.*1760.

Scallop, Scalloped In the shape of a shell, with a rim indented like a sea shell.

Scratch blue Scratched or incised ornament with colour showing only in incisions.

Sealtop Cast finial of early spoons with flat top resembling a sealing-wax seal.

Seat board The wooden board on which the movement rests in longcase clocks.

Seaweed marquetry Patterns of intricate scrolling veneer.

Secretaire Fitted writing compartment with hinged fall-front, sometimes pulling out like a drawer. Also the whole piece of writing furniture incorporating this desk fitting.

Serpentine Front of furniture with horizontal S-curve.

Sèvres Famous French porcelain factory succeeding Vincennes in 1756, producing hard-paste porcelain from *c.*1772, soft-paste earlier.

Sgraffito See Scratch blue.

Sham See Dummy.

Sheffield plate Method of coating a copper core with thin layer of sterling silver, heat-fused and then worked like silver, with cut edges masked with great skill. From *c.*1742.

Shoe The brass fitting on furniture leg into which castor was fixed.

Shoulder knop The first knop below the bowl of a glass, or the socket of a candlestick.

Side chair Made to stand against a wall, armless chair usually slightly lower and wider than dining chair.

Silesian stem In glass, cut or shaped with four, six or eight sides tapering inwards below pronounced shoulder knop.

Sinking Shaping a piece of sheet silver by hammering in a hollowed out wooden block into a bowl shape.

Slice cutting Deep V-shaped incisions in glass.

Slipware Coarse earthenware covered or decorated with slip, watered-down potters' clay.

Smith's blue Brilliant blue underglaze named after its developer.

Snap-top Table with top which hinges from horizontal to vertical secured by small snap-hinge.

Snuffers Scissor-like implement with small box on one blade for extinguishing and trimming wicks of candles.

Soapstone porcelain Soft-paste porcelain with a steatite content, hot-water resistant and tougher than soft-paste porcelain.

Soda glass Used by Venetians, quick-cooling malleable glass often straw coloured or green tinged, and bubbled, more fragile than English flint glass.

Soft-paste porcelain White, translucent paste made in England from $c.$1740s.

Spade foot Square-sectioned tapering foot.

Spandrel Corner-piece, usually decorative, on clocks, furniture.

Spill jar Wide-mouthed often straight-sided vase.

Spindle turned Wood tapering at either end, swelling slightly in centre.

Spire cut In the shape of a church spire or steeple.

Splat Central vertical piece of chairback, often with decorative shape, ornament.

Splash enamel Opaque or coloured enamel splashed on to glass while still in molten state.

Spun silver Method of cheap, swift shaping of thin-gauge objects in silver and other metals, mainly 19th century.

Staffordshire Pottery from main centre of British pottery industry, loose term for brightly-painted earthenware and flat-backed mantel ornaments.

Sterling silver Pure silver alloyed with small quantity of copper to the standard required by Assay Offices.

Staved Decoration, construction, like a fence.

Stipple engraving See Diamond-point engraving.

Stirrup cup Round-based cup, usually in the shape of fox's head or other animal, used by mounted horsemen before a hunt.

Stoneware Earthenware mixed with sand or flint and fired at a higher temperature, making it non porous and strong.

Stourbridge glass Usually refers to glass made after $c.$1845 when new industrial glass centre was Stourbridge, noted for glassmaking from 17th century onwards.

Strapwork Low relief applied or carved, of scrolls, arabesques, geometric motifs, and in silver, applied ornament.

Stretcher Horizontal rails between the legs of tables, chairs, to give extra stability and strength.

Strike/silent Small lever or dial on clock face for regulating strike mechanism.

Strawberry dish Small saucer-like bowl, usually with fluted sides.

Stringing Narrow strips of wood or brass inlaid in wood. In glass, glass threads wound in spirals round stems, handles, etc.

Stuff-over Furniture frame, seat frame, covered with upholstery.

Sulphide glass Small china clay portraits in low relief embedded in brilliant flint glass, developed by Apsley Pellatt $c.$1819.

Sunderland Centre of earthenware pottery, known for making nautical and marine commemorative ware, mainly 19th century.

Glossary

Sunray veneer Cut in narrow triangular sections resembling rays of sun.
Swag Heavy curve of drapery, fruit, flowers.

Tallboy Double chest of drawers made in two parts from *c.*1710.
Tambour Flexible desk top or sliding cabinet door made of upright concave batons glued to thick fabric.
Tapered Narrowing towards the base.
Tazza From Italian meaning 'cup' on a tall stem. Misused as a type of silver tray or salver.
Tear drop Bubble of air entrapped in stem of glass.
Terminal Literally the end, usually of decorative socket or base of handle, etc.
Thumb moulding Flattened half-round moulding on edges of furniture, round drawer fronts.
Timepiece Any clock with no striking mechanism.
Tin enamel, tin glaze Once-fired earthenware dipped in lead glaze mixed with tin oxide giving a smooth white finish.
Toastmaster's glass Glass with thick bowl to exaggerate quantity of liquor.
Tower clock, turret clock Large clocks made for steeples, churches, stable buildings, etc.
Train The wheels and pinions forming the movement of a clock.
Transfer printing Pattern transferred to ceramic on tissue paper.
Trefid, trifid Three lobed, as trefoil.
Trembleuse Saucer with raised central rim to hold cup in centre.
Tudric pewter With a shine like silver, used for 'Art Nouveau' wares from *c.*1902.
Tunbridge ware Marquetry boxes of 17th century and parquetry from *c.*1800.
Turned, turning Timber, metal, etc. shaped on a lathe in symmetrical circular motifs.
Twin train clock With a going train for movement and a striking train for chime.
Twist turned Asymmetrical turning of wood, etc. in barley-sugar twist.

Underglaze Pattern, colour, decoration applied to once-fired pottery and porcelain and then glazed.
Useful wares Denotes all but decorative and cabinet wares in pottery and porcelain.

Vandyke rim Scalloped like lace.
Veneer Thin sheets of wood shaped, cut and glued to carcase.
Verge escapement See Escapement.
Vesta case Match case.
Vinaigrette Small box with tightly fitting lid to hold scrap of aromatic sponge.
Vincennes Forerunner to famous Sèvres porcelain factory.
Vitreous Glass-like, with glass-like properties.
Vitruvian scroll Formalized S-scroll in wave pattern.
Volute Spiral scroll.

Glossary

Waisted Straight or cylindrical shape curving inward like an hourglass.

Waiter A salver or tray.

Whatnot Tall extended form of dumb waiter with open shelves in tiers on central pillar or slender legs.

Wheel engraving Designs cut in glass with a revolving wheel and abrasive powder.

Whieldon, Thomas Staffordshire potter noted for development of marbled and mingled clays and glazes.

Williamite Period when William of Orange ruled alone from 1694–1702. Also in glass, period following Battle of the Boyne and establishment of Orange Order from *c.*1780.

Willow pattern Pseudo-Chinese design popularly used on early 19th-century pottery for tablewares.

Winding square The square, often shuttered, into which a clock key is inserted.

Windsor chair Hoop-backed solid wood chair, never veneered, with saddle seat, made in elm, oak, yew wood.

Wine cistern Large containers filled with ice or cold water in silver, marble, or lead or zinc-lined mahogany, often with a tap at the bottom to let out water.

Wine cooler Smaller versions of cisterns, often made in pairs for sideboards, in silver, mahogany, etc.

Wine taster Small, shallow, two-handled or two-eared bowl, usually Scottish or French, from 17th century.

Zaffre Saxony cobalt, blue pigment used for ceramic decoration from *c.*1545.

Bibliography

Furniture
Beard, Geoffrey. *National Trust Book of English Furniture.*
Viking in association with the National Trust.
Duncan, Alastair. *Art Nouveau Furniture.* Thames & Hudson.
Feild, Rachael. *Buying Antique Furniture.* Macdonald & Co.
(Publishers) Ltd.
Fleming, John. *The Penguin Dictionary of Decorative Arts.*
Gloag, John. *A Short Dictionary of Furniture.* George Allen &
Unwin.
Lucie Smith, Edward. *Furniture: a Concise History.* Thames &
Hudson.
Savage, George. *Dictionary of 19th century Antiques.* Barrie &
Jenkins.
Wills, Geoffrey. *English Furniture.* Guinness Superlatives Ltd.

Clocks
Barker, David. *The Arthur Negus Guide to English Clocks.*
Hamlyn.
Bird, Anthony. *English House Clocks 1600–1850.* David &
Charles.
Brewer, Clifford. *The Country Life Collector's Pocket Book of
Clocks.*
Loomes, Brian. *Complete British Clocks.* David & Charles.
Nicholls, A. *Clocks in Colour.* Blandford Press.
Smith, Alan. *The Guinness Book of Clocks.* Guinness
Superlatives Ltd.
Symonds, R. W. *A History of English Clocks.* King Penguin.

Silver
Bannister, Judith. *The Country Life Collector's Pocket Book of
Silver.*
Clayton, Michael. *The Collector's Dictionary of Silver and Gold.*
Culme, John. *Nineteenth-Century Silver.*
Luddington, John. *Starting to Collect Silver.* Antique
Collectors' Club.
Rowe, Robert. *Adam Silver 1765 to 1795.*
Wardle, Patricia. *Victorian Silver and Silver-Plate.*
Wills, Geoffrey. *The Guinness Book of Silver.* Guinness
Superlatives Ltd.

Pottery and Porcelain
Bembrose, G. *19th Century English Pottery & Porcelain.*
Fay-Hallé, A. and Barbara Mundt. *19th century European
porcelain.* Trefoil Books Ltd.
Fisher, S. W. *English Pottery & Porcelain Marks.* W. Foulsham
& Co.
Godden, Geoffrey. *Encyclopaedia of British Pottery & Porcelain.*
Hughes, G. Bernard. *The Country Life Collector's Pocket Book of
China.*

Bibliography

Spero, Simon. *Worcester Porcelain*. Lund Humphries
Publications.
Wills, Geoffrey. *English Pottery and Porcelain*. Guinness
Superlatives Ltd.

Glass
Haynes, E. B. *Glass through the Ages*. Penguin Books.
Lattimore, Colin R. *English 19th Century Press-Moulded Glass*.
Barrie and Jenkins.
Newman, Harold. *Illustrated Dictionary of Glass*.
Vane Percy, C. *The Glass of Lalique*. Trefoil Books Ltd.
Wills, Geoffrey. *English and Irish Glass*. Guinness Superlatives
Ltd.
Wills, Geoffrey. *The Country Life Collector's Pocket Book of
Glass*.

Colour Section

Art Deco figure xiii

Baccarat xv
bellringer's jug xii
Bloor Derby xi
brass and enamel vi
bureau-bookcase ii

Canterbury i
Carlton House type iv
carriage clocks vi, vii
centre table iii
claret jugs viii
cottage models xi
cow creamer ix

decanters viii
Derby xii
dining chairs iv

elbow chairs i

French gilt vi, vii

goblets xiv

mantle clock v
marble iii, v
models xi
mounted clock vii

ormolu iii, v

paperweights xiv, xv
pot and cover xi

ruby glass xiv

salt-glaze xii
sheep models xii
Sheraton period i
St. Louis xiv

tankard xvi
tea caddy ix

vases xv, xvi

whatnot i
wine labels x
writing tables iii, iv

Index

Adam Brothers 18, 22
Adam period 32
Act of Parliament Clock 100
air-twist 239, 249, 250
ale glasses 255, 256
anchor escapement 102
antique dealers 9
antique fairs, markets 10
apostle spoons 169
architects' table 69
armoires 83–85
Art Deco 132, 236
Art Nouveau 19, 136, 178
Arts and Crafts Movement
    13, 19, 84, 136
Assay Office 137, 138
aumbry 75
authenticity 19, 20

bachelor's chest 82
bachelor's tea set 167
ball and claw 29, 30
balloon-back chair 38
balloon clocks 128
baluster glass 240, 247, 248
basalt 176
basaltes 220
basting spoons 170
Bateman, Hester 140, 145
bellarmine 186
Belleek 209
bergeres 27
biggin 163
Bingham, Edward 179
Bloor Derby 217
'blue and white' 184, 190,
    191
bone china 180, 206, 213
bonheur du jour 73
Boulle 130
Boulton, Matthew 140, 147
Bow 176, 190, 194, 195,
    204, 218
boxes (silver) 173
bracket clocks 97, 99,
    118–124
brass inlay, marquetry 19

breakfast table 46, 47
breakfront 92
Bristol 205
Britannia Standard 137
bureaux 67, 68
bureau-bookcase 65
bureau-cabinets 63, 64

cabbage leaf jug 194, 205
cabinet-makers 22
cabinet ware 215, 221
cabriole legs 28, 29, 30, 77,
    78
caddy spoons 168
cake baskets 152, 153
cameo glass 261, 262, 264
candlesticks 148, 149, 218
carcase 18, 20, 81
card tables 52–54
Carlton House desk 72
Carolean antiques 21, 24
carriage clocks 99, 126, 127
casters 143
Castle Heddingham 179
Caughley 207, 211
centre table 60
centrepieces 219
chairs 21–39
chambersticks 147
character jugs 235
Chelsea 176, 179, 193, 194,
    197, 198–200
chest on stand 61
chestnut warmers 203
chests 74
chest of drawers 80–82,
    86–88
cheverets 73
chiffoniers 96
'Chinese' taste 31
chinoiserie 18, 31, 55, 135,
    183, 184
chip carving 17
Chippendale period, style 9,
    12, 18, 22, 30, 32, 55, 65
claret jugs 159, 243
Cliff, Clarice 178, 236

Index

clock casework 98
clock makers 100
Coalbrookdale 218
Coalport 180, 212
coasters 160
coffee cans 190
coffee pots 162, 163
coffers 74
colour twist glass 252
commission bids (salerooms) 11
commodes 86, 89
Commonwealth silver 141
conditions of sale 10, 11
Cooper, Susie 178
Copeland 180
cordial glasses 247, 251, 256
Craftsmen Potters 179
country furniture 12, 13, 18, 19, 20, 28, 90, 91
court cupboard 75
cream jugs 145
creamers 145
creamware 176, 195, 204
credence table 41
Cushion, John 179
cut glass 239, 242, 243

damage 180, 181
Davenport (pottery) 212
davenport desk 71
decanters 238, 242
deceptive glasses 246
Delftware 182–184
demilune 53, 59
Derby 176, 177, 180, 203, 211
Derbyshire Chair 23
desks, writing furniture 69–73
dessert plates 214
dessert services 210–213
dishes (silver) 150, 155
Doulton 178, 181, 224
draw-leaf table 41
Dresden 178, 179
dressers 90, 91
drop-leaf table 43
drug jars 182
drum table 50
dumb waiter 55

Early English silver 141, 142
Edwardian antiques 9, 13, 136
electioneering glass 251
electroplate 136
electrotype 137
Elizabethan revival 13
engraved glass 238, 239, 245, 251, 253, 254, 257
escritoire 61
estimates (salerooms) 11
ewers 159, 226, 263

'fairyland lustre' 178, 223
fakes and forgeries (silver) 138
'fauteuils' 33
firing glass 246
flatware (silver) 171, 172
Flaxman, John 135, 137
flint glass 8, 237
Fromanteel, John 97, 100
fruit dish 150
furniture designers 22

Galle 264
games table 52–54
Garnier, Paul 99
garnitures 216, 217
gateleg table 42
glass tax 239
goblets 158, 244, 245
Godden, Geoffrey 179
Gothic 19, 66, 75, 93, 99, 129, 233

hallmarks 137
hard-paste porcelain 176, 205, 206
harlequin table 57
Heal, Ambrose 22, 38
Hepplewhite style, period 9, 18, 22, 34
Honey, William 179
housekeeper's cupboard 84
Huguenot silversmiths 134

'improving' 138
Irish glass 239

Jacobean 19
Jacobite glass 246, 253, 254
Japan pattern 202, 208, 209
japanning 18
jasper ware 221, 222
Jones, George 178
jugs 205, 243

Kent, William 18, 22
kneehole 79
Knibb, J. 98, 100

lacquer 18, 105, 108, 113, 119, 120
ladies' desks 72, 73
ladles 170
Lalique 265
Lambeth pottery 178

lantern clocks 101, 102
Leach, Bernard 179
lead glass 8, 237
leaf dish 194, 200
legal protection 9
library bookcases 92, 93
library tables 48–50
Liverpool 176, 183, 188, 190, 195, 204
livery cupboard 75
London clocks 97, 98, 112–117
longcase clocks 97, 105–117
Longton Hall 181, 190, 197, 203
lowboys 77, 78
Lowestoft 176, 185, 188, 191

machines 18
Mackintosh, C. R. 22, 84
mahogany 18–20
majolica ware 177, 178
Makeig-Jones, Daisy 178
mantel clocks 130, 131
Marot, Daniel 22, 24
marquetry 17
Martin Brothers 179
McKinley Tariff Act 180
Meisson 200
Minton 178, 180, 216
monteiths 154
Moorcroft MacIntyre 225
Moorcroft pottery 224
mortise and tenon 17
mote spoons 168
mugs 156, 157, 204

Nailsea glass 239
Nantgarw 177
Newcastle glass 238
New Hall 177, 205, 206

oak 17–21, 23, 40, 41
Oakley, George 92
occasional table 60
ormolu 19, 89, 130, 131

Palladian 18
panelled construction 17, 23, 74
paperweights 259
'parian' 177
parquetry 18
partners' desks 69, 70
pastille burners 232, 233
pearlware 176, 210
pedestal desks 69, 70
Pembroke tables 57, 58
periods, dates and styles 9, 12, 14–17, 134, 239

pillar-and-claw 44, 45
pine 18–20
Pinxton 204
'plate' 133
polychrome 185
porcelain 175
porringer 142
potteries 180, 181
presses 83, 84
prices 21, 101, 139, 182, 241
provincial 9, 12, 35, 138
provincial clocks 98, 105–111, 121
punch bowl 154

quarter veneer 67
quartetto table 56
'Queen Anne' 9, 12, 25, 28, 63, 67, 81–83, 114, 134,136, 143, 157, 165

Ravenscroft, George 237
refectory table 40
Regency period 18, 19, 177
registration marks 180
regulator clocks 99, 125
rent table 50
reserves (salerooms) 11
restoration 181
Rockingham 181, 215
Rococo 135, 192, 193
'roemer' 238, 245
rose bowl 154
Royal Crown Derby 180
Royal Doulton 178
Royal Worcester 178, 179, 181

sabre leg 37
salerooms 8, 10
salt-glaze 175, 185, 186
salts 144
salvers 151
sauce boats 146, 192, 193
scent bottles 174
sealtop spoons 169
secretaire 62
serving table 55, 56
sheep's head clock 102
Sheffield Assay Office 9
Sheffield plate 9, 136
Sheraton period, style 9, 18, 22, 35, 86, 135
shield back 34
ship bowl 183
sideboards 94, 95
sidereal time 99
side tables 76
silversmiths 133, 140
silver table 55